DAKSHIN BHOG

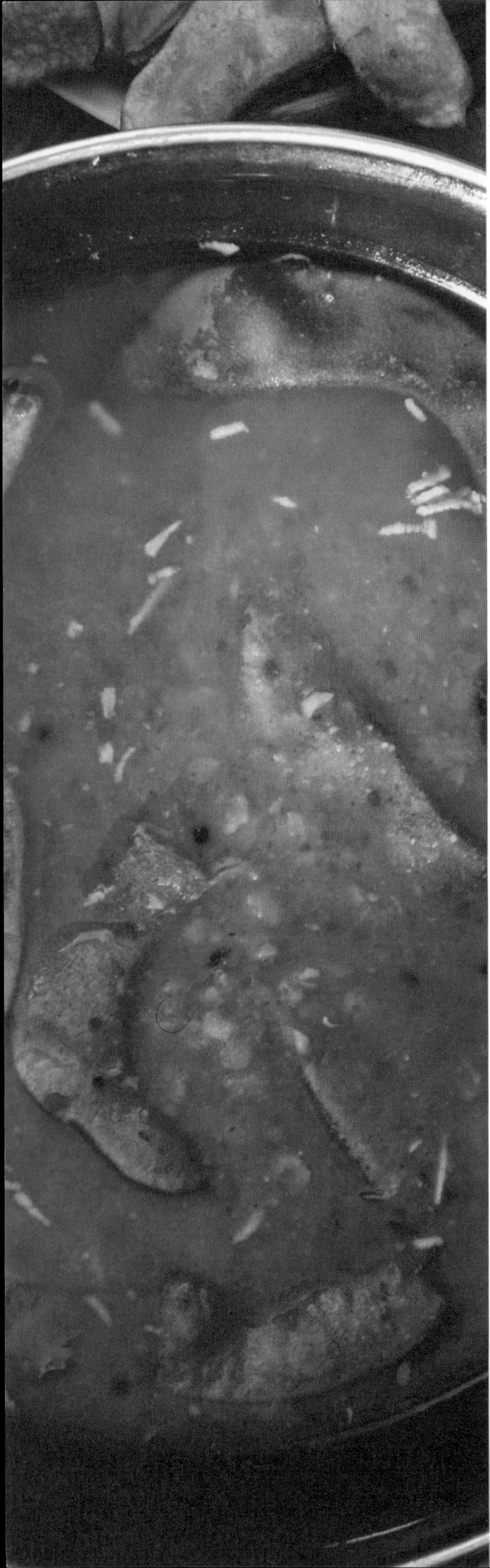

First Published 2007
Second Impression 2008

Published by
Rupa & Co
7/16 Ansari Road, Daryaganj
New Delhi 110 002

Sales Centres:
Allahabad Bangalooru Chandigarh Chennai
Hyderabad Jaipur Kathmandu Kolkata
Mumbai

Book design by Sonali Lal

Photographs on page 8, 14, 24, 25, 26, 30, 37, 90, 98, 101, 103, 120, 129, 132, 133, 136 by
Om Photos, SA Rajgopal
Venue: The Park Sheraton Hotel, Chennai

Printed in India by
Brijbasi Art Press Ltd., Noida

DAKSHIN BHOG

Flavours of South Indian Cooking

Santhi Balaraman

Photography by Karan Khanna

Rupa & Co

contents

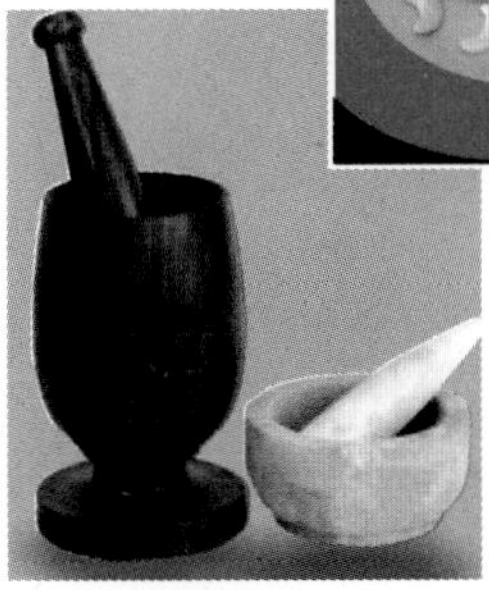

A good menu is like a good story. It must have a proper balance of dramatic elements, sorted out and arranged in a coherent manner. All elements must be resolved in the end, for unlike some stories, all meals must have only happy endings.

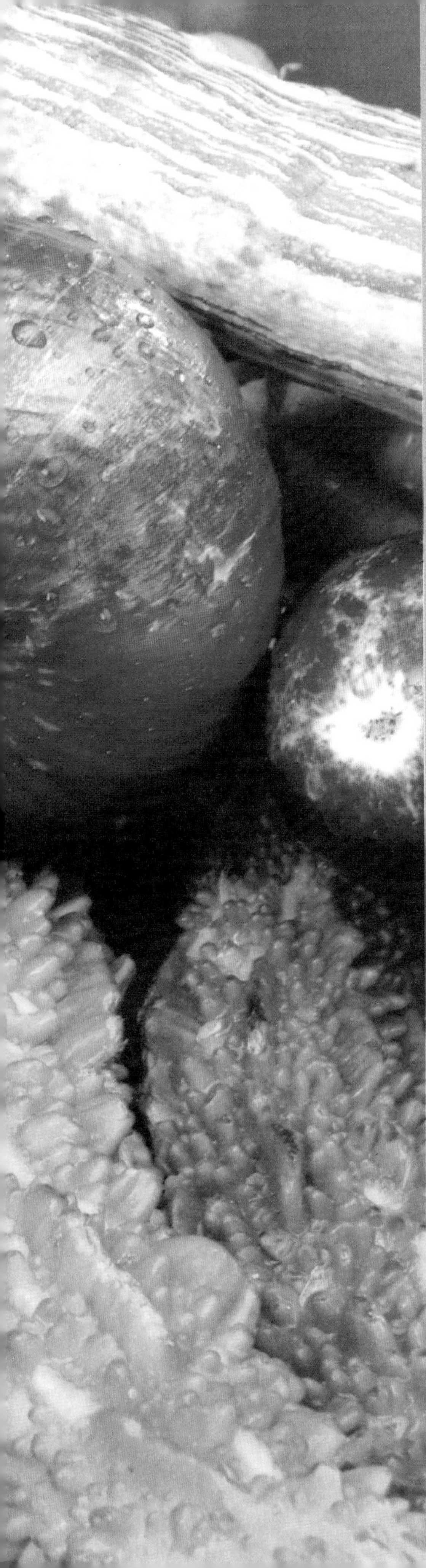

Introduction

Health and happiness is wealth, most people would agree. Good food plays a very important part in this: A well-fed family is likely to be a happy and healthy family also.

Our traditional recipes have been time tested by generations and proven to be healthy, nutritious and very tasty. The invasion of fast food is slowly pushing our traditional cooking into the background. However, fast food caters only to one's taste, not to one's health. The preconception in young families today is that traditional cooking is tedious and time-consuming. While this might have been true until a few years ago, today modern facilities and gadgets have greatly simplified traditional recipes. In this book, an attempt has been made to revive traditional recipes, even if in a small way.

Indian cooking has a very rich history, as diverse and varied as its culture. Each region has its own unique cuisine with its special blends of spices and methods depending on location, climate and lifestyle. This book, of course, is not exhaustive; it includes about 250 traditional recipes, mostly from Tamil Nadu and a few from other southern states. Care has been taken to select only simple recipes, modifying the method if need be, and to cover all categories of cuisine: breakfast, lunch, tiffin, snacks and sweets. Ingredients have been selected keeping in mind their nutritional value and easy availability. Good food does not necessarily mean expensive and rich food. It means economical food. A cook should be able to produce interesting and nutritious meals with minimum expense and time. All the recipes are tested and measurements checked in my kitchen, which is also my lab.

Before you step into the kitchen, a few points should be noted. Traditional preparations usually use local vegetables like brinjal, raw banana, ladies finger, broad beans and a variety of greens. Any other vegetables can be added or substituted in the given recipes if desired. Measurements given in this book are to serve about four persons generally, unless mentioned otherwise. Also, the names of all recipes are given in Tamil unless mentioned otherwise. I have added a glossary of terms used in English, Hindi, Tamil at the end.

Any feedback and suggestions are welcome.

Santhi Balaraman

TIFFIN MEALS

Traditionally, in many parts of south India, it is quite common to have a mid-morning lunch around eleven o' clock, and then a 'tiffin' meal around five in the evening. However, now-a-days, this is no longer common, especially among the younger generation. In any case, these recipes are also prepared for breakfast.

Research has shown that a south Indian breakfast is one of the most nutritious and easily digestible. Most of the dishes are made out of fermented rice and/or a mixture of rice and dhal. Fermented rice is supposed to be very good for digestion when consumed in the morning. Also, it has been proved that south Indian breakfasts combine the correct amounts of carbohydrate and protein for a balanced meal. This provides the required energy and nutrition to start the day. Therefore, recipes like idli, pongal, etc. are highly recommended by doctors even for children and recuperating patients.

Idli

Idli

(STEAMED RICE CAKE)

Ingredients

Parboiled rice	*2 cups*
Whole urad dhal	*½ cup*
Salt	*to taste*

Method

Wash and soak rice and urad dhal separately for 4 to 5 hours. First grind the rice coarsely in a grinder. Remove and keep aside. Then grind the urad dhal (sprinkling water now and then) for about 30 minutes till it becomes fluffy. Mix the ground rice, urad dhal and required salt well. Transfer to a large vessel and keep aside. Allow to ferment for 10-15 hours. Mix again thoroughly. Now the idli batter is ready for use. As and when required, prepare idlis.

Grease idli plate with a little oil. Pour 1 ladle of batter into each idli mould. Steam in idli cooker for 10-15 minutes (If pressure cooker is used for steaming, the cooker weight should not be used).

Pachaipairu Idli

(MOONG DHAL IDLI)

Method

In this recipe, rice is not used. Equal portions of moong dhal and urad dhal are ground together to prepare the batter. Idlis are prepared in the same way as in previous recipe. There is no need for the batter to ferment or be soaked.

Note

Recommended for diabetics.

Rava Idli

(SEMOLINA IDLI)

Ingredients

Rava	*3 cups*
Sour curd	*3 cups*
Green chilli paste	*2 tsp*
Coriander leaves	*2 tbsp, chopped*
Salt	*to taste*
Gingelly oil	*as required*
To season	
Mustard seeds	*½ tsp*
Urad dhal	*1 tsp*
Channa dhal	*1 tsp*

Method

Dry roast rava. Soak it in the curd, mix in the required salt and keep aside. Heat oil in a kadai, lightly fry the seasonings and add to the rava mixture. Mix in chilli paste and coriander (if required also add a pinch of cooking soda). Prepare like other idlis and steam up to 8 minutes in idli cooker.

Rava Idli

Semiya Idli

(VERMICELLI IDLI)

Method

This is prepared in the same way as rava idli, using vermicelli instead of rava.

Venthia Idli

(FENUGREEK IDLI)

Ingredients

Parboiled rice	*2 cups*
Fenugreek seeds	*2½ tsp*
Salt	*to taste*

Method

Wash and soak rice and fenugreek seeds for at least 3 hours. Grind together well for a minimum of 1 hour (with required water) till the batter is soft and frothy. Mix required salt and transfer to a large vessel. Allow the batter to ferment for at least 15 hours. Prepare idlis as usual in idli cooker as and when needed.

Note

Recommended for diabetics.

Kanchipuram Idli

Ingredients

Raw rice	*2 cups*
Urad dhal	*1¾ cup*
Pepper	*2 tsp, crushed*
Jeera	*2 tsp*
Curd	*½ litre*
Ghee	*a little*
Salt	*to taste*
Gingelly oil	*as required*

Method

Wash and soak rice and urad dhal separately for 4 to 5 hours. Grind as per recipe for idli. Transfer to a large vessel and mix required salt. Allow to ferment for 10-15 hours. As and when required, add ghee, oil, pepper, jeera and curd and mix well. Smear oil in small metal cups or tumblers and fill them half with this batter. Arrange in idli cooker and steam like idlis for 15 minutes till done.

Idiaappam

(SOFT RICE NOODLES)

Ingredients

Processed rice flour	*1 cup*
Salt	*to taste*
Gingelly oil	*1 tsp*

Method

Boil 2 cups of water. Add required salt and oil. Slowly mix rice flour in the boiling water, constantly stirring so that lumps are not formed. After 2 minutes put off the flame. When it is cooled, knead the dough to make it soft (if required warm water can be sprinkled). Roll into cylindrical balls. Grease the inside of the idiaappam press mould. Keep one ball in the mould and press it in a circular motion on an idli plate. Steam cook for 5 minutes. Transfer to a greased tray immediately. Repeat the same with the rest of the dough. Idiaappam is well accompanied with plain coconut milk or kai kurma or potato stew. (See 'Crispy Snacks' for preparation of processed rice flour.)

Aappam

(SOFT DOSA)

Ingredients

Raw rice	*2 cups*
Parboiled rice	*1 tbsp*
Urad dhal	*1 tbsp*

Baking soda	*a pinch*
Grated coconut	*1 tbsp, optional*
Coconut milk	*2½ cups*
Sugar	*2 tsp*
Salt	*to taste*
Oil	*as required*

Method

Wash and soak rice and dhal for 2-3 hours. Grind to a very fine batter with required water. Mix required salt and a pinch of baking soda. Allow this batter to ferment for more than 24 hours. Just before preparing aappam, add 2 tsp of sugar and mix well. Add also 2 cups of thick coconut milk and half cup diluted coconut milk (the batter should be in a consistency that allows you to pour it). Heat a shallow kadai (aappam kadai) and smear the inside with a little oil. Pour the batter with a ladle, around the edge of kadai in a circular motion, in such a way that the batter spreads up to the middle of the kadai to form a dosa. Keep the kadai covered with a lid till it is done. The edge of the aappam should be thin and crispy and the middle should be thick and soft. There is no need to turn over the aappam to the other side. Serve aappam with sweet coconut milk or kai kurma or stew.

Dosai

(RICE PANCAKE)

Ingredients

Parboiled rice	*2 cups*
Whole urad dhal	*¼ cup*
Fenugreek seeds	*½ tsp, optional*
Salt	*to taste*
Oil	*as required*

Method

Wash and soak the above ingredients together (except oil) for 4 hours. Grind well to a smooth batter. Leave it for 4-5 hours. Add water if required and prepare dosas as and when needed using a little oil.

Vengaya Oothappam

(THICK DOSA WITH ONION)

Ingredients

Parboiled rice	*2 cups*
Whole urad dhal	*½ cup*
Toor dhal	*1 tbsp*
Fenugreek seeds	*2 tsp*
Onion	*2, very finely chopped*
Garlic	*2, grated*
Ginger	*1" piece, grated*
Coriander leaves	*a few, finely chopped*
Green chillies	*2, finely chopped*
Salt	*to taste*
Oil	*as required*

Method

Soak rice, dhals and fenugreek seeds together for 4 hours and grind well to a soft batter. Mix in required salt. Leave it to ferment for a minimum of 20 hours. As and when required, prepare thick dosas on a dosa tawa. Pour 1 tsp oil around the dosa. Cover with a lid. Open the lid after 30 seconds. Sprinkle finely chopped onion, green chilli, ginger, garlic, coriander leaves on top of the oothappam. Turn over to the other side carefully. Cook on a medium flame till both sides are done.

Note

This can also be prepared without onion. Instead of onion, a combination of grated carrot, greens or any other vegetable can also be used.

Masal Dosai

(DOSA WITH POTATO FILLING)

Ingredients

Parboiled rice	*2 cups*
Raw rice	*½ cup*
Rava	*2 tsp*
Urad dhal	*½ cup*
Salt	*to taste*
Oil	*as required*
Prepared filling	*as required.*
For filling	
Potato	*4, boiled, peeled and mashed*
Onion	*2, finely chopped*
Green chillies	*3 to 4, chopped*
Turmeric powder	*1 tsp*
Chilli powder	*1 tsp*
Mustard seeds	*½ tsp*
Urad dhal	*½ tsp*
Curry leaves	*a few*
Salt	*to taste*
Oil	*as required*

To prepare filling

Heat 1 tsp oil and lightly fry mustard seeds, urad dhal and curry leaves. Then add green chillies and onion and shallow fry. Add potatoes and mash together. Mix turmeric powder, chilli powder and required salt in a little water. Add this to the potato and boil together till the mixture takes on a thick consistency.

Method

Wash and soak all ingredients (except oil) for 4 hours and grind together well to a soft batter. Allow to ferment for a minimum of 6-8 hours. Add water, if required, to the batter. Prepare thin dosas, as and when required, on a dosa tawa, using little oil. When the bottom becomes crisp, spread a little filling on the dosa and fold it into a semicircle. Serve hot with chutney and sambar.

Note

Fresh green peas or any other desired vegetables can also be combined with the potato filling.

Rava Dosai

(SEMOLINA DOSA)

Ingredients

Rava	*1 cup*
Rice flour	*1 cup*
Maida	*½ cup*
Onion	*1, finely chopped*
Green chillies	*2, finely chopped*
Ginger	*1″ piece, grated*
Curry leaves	*a few*
Jeera	*1 tsp*
Pepper corn	*½ tsp*
Salt	*to taste*
Oil	*as required*

Method

Soak rava, rice flour and maida together with salt in water for 2-3 hours. Mix in onions, green chillies, ginger, curry leaves, jeera and pepper. Add required water to make a thin batter. Heat a dosa tawa, pour the batter from the outer edge towards the centre, with a cup (do not spread the batter with a ladle). Pour 1 tsp of oil around the dosa. Cook on medium flame on both sides till the dosa is crisp and golden brown.

Rava Dosai

Masal Dosai

Gothumai Dosai

(INSTANT DOSA)

Ingredients

Wheat flour	*1 cup*
Rice flour	*½ cup*
Maida	*½ cup*
Green chillies	*2, finely chopped*
Ginger	*1" piece, finely chopped*
Curry leaves	*a few*
Pepper corn	*½ tsp*
Salt	*to taste*
Oil	*as required*

Method

Mix well all the above ingredients together (except oil) with required water to make a thin batter. There is no need for the batter to ferment or soak. Dosas can be prepared immediately. Prepare like rava dosai.

Vella Dosai

(SWEET DOSA)

Ingredients

Wheat flour	*1 cup*
Rice flour	*½ cup*
Powdered jaggery	*½ cup*
Cardamom powder	*1 tsp*
Salt	*a pinch*
Oil	*as required*

Method

Soak both flours in 2 cups of water. Dissolve jaggery in a little water and mix it in the batter. Add cardamom powder and salt (the batter should be in pouring consistency). Prepare like rava dosai.

Pesarettu (Andhra)

Adai

(THICK COARSE DOSA)

Ingredients

Parboiled rice	*2 cups*
Channa dhal	*¾ cup*
Toor dhal	*¾ cup*
Green chilli	*4*
Red chilli	*4*
Asafoetida	*2 pinches*
Curry leaves	*a few*
Salt	*to taste*
Oil	*as required*

Method

Soak rice and dhals separately for 3 hours. Coarsely grind the rice together with green chillies, red chillies and asafoetida. Add and coarsely grind the dhals into this mixture. Mix in required salt and curry leaves. Heat tawa and prepare adais like thick dosas using 2 tsp of oil.

Note

Finely chopped onion, garlic and ginger can be added to the batter.

Chopped fenugreek leaves, drumstick leaves or any other greens can also be used.

Grated coconut (2 tbsp) can also be ground into the mixture.

Pesarettu (Andhra)

(MOONG DHAL DOSA)

To prepare batter

Whole moong dhal	*2 cups*
Rice	*½ cup*
Red chillies	*4*
Green chillies	*4*
Jeera	*1 tsp*
Salt	*to taste*
Oil	*as required*

Soak rice and dhal together for 4 hours. Grind together with chillies, jeera and required salt to a coarse thick batter. Mix well. Keep aside.

To prepare filling

Ginger	*1" piece*
Red chillies	*6*
Whole urad dhal	*1 tbsp*
Tamarind	*a little*
Copra	*1 tbsp*

Fry in oil and grind the above with required salt to make a coarse ginger paste.

Onions	*3, finely chopped*
Coriander leaves	*1 cup, finely chopped*
Asafoetida	*a pinch*
Cashew nuts	*1 tbsp*
Salt	*to taste*
Oil	*as required*

Heat a little oil. Shallow fry onions, coriander leaves, asafoetida and cashew nuts. Mix in ground ginger paste and shallow fry for a few minutes. This is used as filling.

To prepare pesarettu

Heat dosa tawa. Spread the batter like a thick dosa. Pour a little oil around it. When the bottom becomes a golden colour, turn over to the other side. After both sides are cooked, turn again and spread 1 tbsp filling on it (rava uppuma can also be used as filling). Fold and serve hot.

Note

Recommended for diabetics.

Venpongal

(RICE AND DHAL KICHADI)

Ingredients

Rice	*1 cup*
Moong dhal	*½ cup*
Pepper corn	*1 tsp*
Jeera	*½ tsp*
Broken cashew nuts	*1 tbsp*
Ginger	*1 tbsp, finely chopped*
Curry leaves	*a few*
Pepper	*½ tsp, crushed*
Salt	*to taste*
Ghee	*as required*

Method

Dry roast dhal for a few minutes. Wash rice and dhal together. Pour 4 cups of water and pressure cook. Keep aside. Fry cashew nuts, pepper and jeera in ghee. Add and fry curry leaves, ginger and crushed pepper. Mix required salt and the fried ingredients in rice mixture. Pour a little ghee on top and serve hot.

Note

Instead of rice, rava can be used to prepare rava pongal.

Venpongal

Gothumai Pongal

(WHEAT PONGAL)

Ingredients

Moong dhal	*½ cup*
Broken wheat rava	*1 cup*
Pepper	*½ tsp*
Cloves	*2*
Jeera	*½ tsp*
Asafoetida	*a pinch*
Turmeric powder	*a pinch*
Salt	*to taste*
Oil	*as required*

Method

Wash and soak moong dhal and broken wheat together. Drain and keep aside. Heat 1 tsp oil in a pressure pan. Lightly fry jeera, pepper, cloves and asafoetida. Add moong dhal and broken wheat. Sauté for 3 minutes. Add turmeric powder, required salt and 3 cups of water. Pressure cook up to 3 whistles or till done. Mix well and serve hot.

Note

Recommended for diabetics.

Sakkari Pongal

(SWEET DHAL AND RICE)

Ingredients

Raw rice	*1 cup*
Moong dhal	*½ cup*
Powdered jaggery	*1¼ cup*
Cashew nuts	*1 tbsp*
Raisins	*1 tbsp*
Cardamom powder	*1 tsp*
Ghee	*as required*

Method

Dry roast dhal and rice in a hot kadai till golden colour. Wash and pressure cook with 4 cups of water. Prepare a jaggery syrup of 1 string consistency. Add 1 tbsp ghee, cardamom powder and then cooked rice. Mix well and cook on a low flame for a few minutes. Fry cashew nuts and raisins in a little ghee and pour this over sweet pongal and serve.

Akkaravadisal

(SWEET RICE AND DHAL)

Ingredients

Moong dhal	*¼ cup*
New raw rice	*¾ cup*
Channa dhal	*1 tsp, optional*
Milk	*4 cups*
Sugar	*2 cups*
Cardamom powder	*a pinch*
Ghee	*as required*

To decorate

Fried almonds, cashew nuts, raisins

Method

Fry dhals and rice in a little ghee till golden colour. Pressure cook in 2 cups of milk and 1 cup of water. Boil the rest of the milk and reduce it to half its original quantity. Add 2 tbsps of ghee, cardamom and cooked rice mixture to the milk and boil for a few more minutes. Mix in sugar gradually, and cook on a low flame. Stir well till the mixture thickens, then decorate. This can be stored for 2 to 3 days.

Thiruvathirai Kali

(SWEET RICE DISH)

Ingredients

Raw rice	*1 cup*
Toor dhal	*3 tbsp*
Grated coconut	*1 cup*
Jaggery	*1 cup*
Cardamom powder	*1 tsp*
Ghee	*as required*

To decorate

Cashew nuts, raisins

Method

Dry roast raw rice and toor dhal separately and grind coarsely. Keep aside. Fry grated coconut slightly and keep aside. Boil jaggery in 1 cup of water in a heavy-bottomed vessel till it takes on a stringy consistency. Add the rice mixture and coconut to this. Add 1 tbsp ghee and cardamom powder (if required, water can also be added). Cook for 20-25 minutes on low flame till done. Decorate with fried cashew nuts and raisins. This is prepared for a special festival called Thiruvathirai for Lord Siva.

Note

The rice and dhal mixture may be pressure-cooked and added to jaggery syrup also. In this case, cook only for 5 to 10 minutes on a low flame.

Arisi Uppuma

(RICE UPPUMA)

Ingredients

Broken rice	*1½ cups*
Toor dhal	*1 tbsp*
Channa dhal	*1 tbsp*
Grated coconut	*½ cup*
Green chillies	*4*
Salt	*to taste*
Oil	*as required*
Coconut oil	*to flavour*

Method

Sieve the broken rice to remove the flour. Soak toor dhal and channa dhal for 10 minutes and grind to a paste. Heat a little oil in a kadai. Lightly fry the seasonings and green chillies. Pour 3 cups of water and add grated coconut, ground dhals and required salt. Bring to a boil. Add broken rice and mix well. Cook for 15-20 minutes, stirring now and then (if required a little hot water can be added). Cook the uppuma on low flame till it is done. Season with mustard seeds, urad dhal, asafoetida and curry leaves.

Puli Uppuma

(SOUR RICE UPPUMA)

Method

The ingredients and method are the same as the recipe for rice uppuma except that, instead of water, thin tamarind extract is used to prepare the sour rice uppuma.

Pidi Uppuma

(UPPUMA ROLLS)

The ingredients are the same as the recipe for rice uppuma except that, in addition, 1 cup of grated snake gourd or bottle gourd is also required.

Method

Soak toor dhal and channa dhal for 10 minutes and grind to a paste. Heat oil in a kadai and fry the seasonings and green chillies. Add grated snake gourd and sauté. Pour in 3 cups of water and add grated coconut and required salt. Bring to boil. Add ground dhals and broken rice, mix well and cook for a few minutes. Remove from fire. When the mixture cools down, divide into small portions and roll into cylinders. Arrange the rolls on idli plates and steam cook in idli cooker till done.

Note

Pidi Uppuma can be prepared without vegetables as well.

Do not sieve the broken rice.

Thavalai Vadai

(UPPUMA VADA)

The ingredients are the same as for rice uppuma.

Method

The rice mixture is prepared as for rice uppuma. Cook the rice mixture only for a few minutes. Remove from fire. After it cools down, divide into small portions. Prepare small vadas. Heat a dosa tawa. Arrange 5-6 vadas on it. Pour a little oil around the vadas. Keep covered with a lid on a reduced flame. When the bottom is done to a golden brown, turn over the vadas. Cook till both sides are crisp.

Note

Do not sieve the broken rice.

Rava Uppuma

(SEMOLINA UPPUMA)

Ingredients

Rava	*2 cups*
Salt	*to taste*
Oil	*as required*
Ghee	*2 tsp*
To season	
Mustard seeds	*½ tsp*
Urad dhal	*1 tsp*
Channa dhal	*1 tsp*
Red chillies	*2, slit*
Green chillies	*2*
Ginger	*1" piece, finely chopped*
Curry leaves	*a few*

Method

In a kadai, roast rava to a golden colour in ghee. Keep aside. Heat 1 tbsp oil. Lightly fry seasonings. Add 3 cups of water and required salt. When the water boils, slowly add the rava, stirring constantly (if required, more hot water can be added). Cook on a low flame till uppuma absorbs all the water and takes on a soft consistency. Decorate with fried cashew nuts.

Puli Uppuma

Gothumai Rava Uppuma

(WHEAT RAVA UPPUMA)

Method

Ingredients and method are the same as for rava uppuma. Instead of rava, broken wheat is used.

Semiya Uppuma

(VERMICELLI UPPUMA)

Method

Ingredients and method are the same as for rava uppuma. Instead of rava, vermicelli is used.

Vengaya Uppuma

(ONION UPPUMA)

Method

Any of the above uppuma can also be prepared with onion.

Kaikari Uppuma

Kaikari Uppuma

(VEGETABLE RAVA UPPUMA)

Method

Any uppuma can be prepared as vegetable uppuma with potatoes, carrot, beans and peas, with or without onion. The vegetables are fried with the seasonings, after which the required water is added. When the vegetables are cooked, add the rava.

Aval Uppuma

(RICE FLAKES UPPUMA)

Ingredients

Rice flakes	*2 cups*
Potatoes	*2, peeled and chopped finely*
Green chillies	*4*
Curry leaves	*a few*
Turmeric powder	*a pinch*
Peanuts	*2 tsp*
Mustard seeds	*1 tsp*
Channa dhal	*1 tsp*
Urad dhal	*1 tsp*
Salt	*to taste*
Oil	*as required*
Chopped coriander leaves	*to decorate*

Method

Wash and soak rice flakes for a few minutes and drain. In a kadai, heat oil. Lightly fry mustard seeds, channa dhal, urad dhal and curry leaves. In the same kadai fry green chillies and then potatoes. Add the peanuts and rice flakes. Shallow fry for 5 minutes. Mix in required salt and turmeric powder. Pour in sufficient water and mix well. Cover and cook till done, and decorate.

Note

Grated mango can be used instead of potato to make mangai aval.

Puli Aval

(SOUR RICE FLAKES UPPUMA)

Method

This is prepared in the same way as aval uppuma but instead of water for cooking, diluted tamarind extract is used.

More Koozh

(BUTTERMILK GRUEL)

Ingredients

Rice flour	*1½ cups*
Sour buttermilk	*1 cup*
Mustard seeds	*1 tsp*
Urad dhal	*1½ tsp*
Green chillies	*3*
Red chillies	*2*
Asafoetida	*a pinch*
Curry leaves	*a few*
Salt	*to taste*
Gingelly oil	*as required*

Method

Mix buttermilk with 3 cups of water. Dissolve the rice flour in this, with required salt. In a kadai, heat 4-5 tsp oil. Let mustard seeds splutter. Add and fry urad dhal, green chillies, red chillies, asafoetida and curry leaves in the same order. Pour in buttermilk mixture, constantly stirring with a wooden ladle. Do not allow lumps to form. When the rice flour is cooked and the mixture becomes creamy, it will turn around the ladle, without sticking. Transfer to a greased tray and spread evenly.

Note

This can also be prepared with wheat flour, maida or sago in the same way.

Puli Koozh

(TAMARIND GRUEL)

Method

Instead of buttermilk, diluted tamarind extract can be used along with all the other ingredients in more koozh to make puli koozh.

Inippu Aappam

(SWEET SOFT DOSA)

Method

Prepare the batter as in the aappam recipe, the previous day. Just before aappams are required, dissolve 1 cup of powdered jaggery in coconut milk and mix it in the batter well. Add a little cardamom powder. Prepare aappams in the same way as in the aappam recipe.

Sevai (Basic)

(RICE VERMICELLI)

Ingredients

Raw rice flour	*½ cup*
Parboiled rice flour	*1 cup*
Salt	*to taste*
Gingelly oil	*as required*

Method

Prepare the dough as for idiaappam. When it is cooled, knead the dough to make it soft (if required water can be sprinkled). Roll into cylindrical balls. Steam the balls in an idli cooker for 8-10 minutes till they are cooked well and become transparent. Meanwhile, grease the inside of a sevai press mould. When the balls are still hot, keep each ball inside the mould and press it on a greased tray, in the shape of vermicelli. Repeat the same with the rest of the dough. Allow this to cool to room temperature without disturbing. This can be served with coconut milk, stew or plain curd. Different kinds of sevais can be prepared from this.

Thengai Sevai

(COCONUT VERMICELLI)

Ingredients

Prepared sevai	*2 cups*
Grated coconut	*½ cup*
Mustard seeds	*1 tsp*
Urad dhal	*1½ tsp*
Red chillies	*2*
Green chillies	*2*
Peanuts and cashew nuts	*1 tsp*
Asafoetida	*a pinch*
Curry leaves	*a few*
Coconut oil	*as required*

Method

In a kadai, lightly fry all the above ingredients except the coconut. Finally add and sauté the coconut to a golden colour. Mix with prepared sevai.

Milagu Sevai

(PEPPER VERMICELLI)

Ingredients

Prepared sevai	*2 cups*
Pepper	*1 tsp*
Jeera	*½ tsp*
Ghee	*as required*

Method

Crush pepper and jeera to a coarse powder and fry in a little ghee. Mix with the prepared sevai. If required, salt can be added.

Puli Sevai

(TAMARIND VERMICELLI)

Method

Mix the prepared sevai with tamarind sauce (prepared as in the recipe for tamarind sauce in the chapter on mixed rice varieties).

Thengai Sevai

Elumicha Sevai

Elumicha Sevai

(LEMON VERMICELLI)

Ingredients

Prepared sevai	*2 cups*
Lemon	*1*
Mustard seeds	*1 tsp*
Urad dhal	*1 tsp*
Channa dhal or fried gram	*1 tsp*
Green chillies	*2*
Turmeric powder	*1 tsp*
Peanuts and cashew nuts	*1 tsp, optional*
Curry leaves	*a few*
Gingelly oil	*as required*

Method

In a kadai, season all the above ingredients. After cooling, squeeze in the lemon. Mix well with the prepared sevai.

Ulutham Sevai

(URAD DHAL VERMICELLI)

Ingredients

Prepared sevai	*2 cups*
Whole urad dhal	*2 tbsp*
Channa dhal	*1 tbsp*
Green chillies	*3*
Mustard seeds	*½ tsp*
Asafoetida	*a pinch*
Curry leaves	*a few*
Salt	*to taste*
Gingelly oil	*as required*

Method

Soak the dhals for 1 hour, drain and grind with required salt and green chillies. Steam this paste in an idli cooker for 10 minutes. After cooling, break it into tiny pieces. In a kadai, lightly fry asafoetida, mustard seeds and curry leaves. Add the steamed dhal. Sauté for a few minutes well. Remove. After cooling, mix this with prepared sevai.

Inippu Sevai

(SWEET VERMICELLI)

Ingredients

Prepared sevai	*2 cups*
Sugar	*½ cup*
Cardamom	*2, powdered*
Cashew nuts	*5, broken*
Saffron colour	*a pinch*
Coconut pieces	*a few*
Ghee	*as required*

Method

In a little ghee, fry cashew nuts and coconut. Keep aside. In a heavy-bottomed kadai, boil sugar in a little water. Add cardamom, colour powder, the fried ingredients and 1 tbsp ghee to this. Allow sugar syrup to develop a hard ball-like consistency. To test, pour 1 tsp of syrup into cold water. This should form a ball when rolled between fingers. Mix the prepared sevai in this and remove from fire.

TIFFIN SNACKS

Tiffin snacks are generally prepared to serve at teatime. These are well known in all parts of the country for their taste. However, most of these snacks are deep fried, so one has to be very careful about the quantity served and consumed.

Sundals are not deep fried and are rich in proteins and fibre. When sprouted, proteins become easily digestible and serve as a whole meal as well.

These snacks are common to all southern states but may be referred to by different names in different places.

Madhur Vadai (Karnataka)

(INSTANT CRISPY VADA)

Ingredients for 20 vadas

Rice flour	*½ cup*
Wheat flour	*½ cup*
Maida	*½ cup*
Rava	*½ cup*
Onion	*1, optional, finely chopped*
Green chillies	*1, optional, finely chopped*
Coriander leaves	*a few, optional, finely chopped*
Curry leaves	*a few*
Salt	*to taste*
Oil	*for deep frying*

Method

Mix all the ingredients (except oil) together in a bowl. Heat oil in a kadai. Add 3 tbsp of hot oil to the flour and blend evenly using your fingertips. Divide flour into small portions. Sprinkle water on one portion to make a stiff dough. Make into large, thin vadas and deep fry in hot oil until crisp and brown. Similarly each portion should be made into a stiff dough and immediately the vadas should be prepared.

Note

Usually crisp madhur vadai are prepared without onion, green chillies, coriander leaves etc.

If all the flours are dry roasted evenly, the vadas become even more crisp.

Sambar Vadai

(VADAS IN HOT GRAVY)

Ingredients

Methu vadas	*10*
Plain sambar	*2 cups (see recipe in gravies)*
Onion	*2, cut*
Green chillies	*2, cut*
Chopped coriander leaves	*to decorate*

Method

Shallow fry green chillies and onion and mix in sambar. Boil for a few minutes. Soak the vadas in the hot sambar for 2 to 3 hours. Arrange on a serving bowl, sprinkle some chopped coriander leaves and serve.

Rasa Vadai

(VADAS IN HOT THIN GRAVY)

Ingredients

Methu vadas	*10*
Paruppu rasam	*2 cups (see recipe in gravies)*
Chopped coriander leaves	*to decorate*

Method

Soak the vadas in hot rasam for 2 to 3 hours. Arrange on a serving bowl, sprinkle some chopped coriander leaves and serve.

Keerai Vadai

(SPINACH VADA)

For 10 vadas

Method

Add finely chopped greens to methu vada batter and prepare vadas likewise.

Note

Finely grated cabbage can be added to the dough to prepare cabbage vada.

Rasa Vadai

Thayir Vadai

(CURD VADA)

Ingredients

Prepared methu vadas	*10*
Thick whipped curd	*2 cups*
Grated coconut	*1 tbsp*
Green chillies	*4*
Salt	*to taste*
Chopped coriander leaves	*to decorate*

Method

Grind coconut and green chillies to a thick paste. Mix this in the curd with required salt in a shallow broad bowl. Dip the vadas in hot water, squeeze out the excess moisture and soak immediately in the curd mixture for 2-3 hours. Arrange in a serving bowl. Pour a little curd on top, sprinkle some chopped coriander leaves and serve.

Note

Do not allow to soak beyond 3 hours otherwise the vadas will become soggy.

Pandigai Vadai

(FESTIVAL VADAI)

Ingredients for 20 vadas

Toor dhal	*½ cup*
Channa dhal	*½ cup*
Whole moong dhal	*½ cup*
Whole urad dhal	*½ cup*
Green chillies	*4, finely chopped*
Coriander leaves	*1 tbsp, finely chopped*
Curry leaves	*1 tbsp, finely chopped*
Ginger	*1 tsp, grated*
Broken cashew nuts	*3 tbsp*
Salt	*to taste*
Oil	*for deep frying*

Method

Clean and soak all the dhals together for 2 or 3 hours. Drain well and grind coarsely with required salt. Mix all the other ingredients. Heat oil in a kadai. Divide the dough into small parts. Flatten each ball into a vada shape on a banana leaf or plastic sheet. Poke a hole in the centre. Deep fry in hot oil till golden brown. This is made for festivals.

Aama Vadai

(CRISPY VADA)

Ingredients for 20 vadas

Channa dhal	*2 cups*
Red chillies	*4*
Green chillies	*4*
Curry leaves	*1 bunch, chopped*
Salt	*to taste*
Oil	*for deep frying*

Method

Clean and soak channa dhal for 3 hours. Drain water and grind with red chillies, green chillies, curry leaves and required salt to a coarse paste. Divide the dough into small parts. Flatten each ball into a vada shape on a banana leaf or plastic sheet. Deep fry in hot oil till golden brown.

Aama Vadai

Thayir Vadai

Masal Vadai

(VADA WITH SPICES)

Ingredients for 20 vadas

Channa dhal	*2 cups*
Garam masala	*1 tsp*
Green chillies	*8, finely chopped*
Ginger	*1 tsp, finely chopped*
Onions	*3, finely chopped*
Curry leaves	*a few, finely chopped*
Coriander leaves	*2 tbsp, finely chopped*
Salt	*to taste*
Oil	*for deep frying*

Method

Clean and soak dhal for 2 hours. Drain water, grind the dhal with required salt to a coarse paste. Mix all other ingredients into the paste. Heat oil in a kadai. Divide the batter into small parts. Flatten each ball into a vada shape on a banana leaf or plastic sheet. Deep fry the prepared vadas in the hot oil till golden brown.

Vazhappoo Vadai

(PLANTAIN FLOWER VADA)

Ingredients for 20 vadas

Plantain flower	*1*
Channa dhal	*1½ cups*
Fried gram	*1 cup*
Green chillies	*8 to 10*
Aniseeds or jeera	*1 tsp*
Turmeric powder	*a pinch*
Onion	*3, optional*
Garlic	*2 flakes, optional*
Salt	*to taste*
Oil	*for deep frying*

Method

Clean and chop plantain flower: remove all the layers of red petals, covering the finger like flowers. Remove also the central stem from each finger like flower. Finally chop all the flowers and keep soaked in thin tamarind extract or butter milk. Drain and add required salt and turmeric powder. Cook in a little water till done. Meanwhile wash and soak channa dhal for 2-3 hours. Drain channa dhal completely, add fried gram, green chillies, (if desired onion and garlic can be added) and required salt. Grind together to a coarse dough. Mix aniseeds and cooked plantain flower into the dough. Prepare small vadas on a plastic sheet. Heat oil in a kadai and deep fry the vadas till golden brown.

Milagu Vadai

(PEPPER VADA)

Ingredients for 20 vadas

Whole urad dhal	*1 cup*
Rice	*1 tbsp*
Pepper corns	*1 tsp, crushed*
Salt	*to taste*
Oil	*for deep frying*

Method

Wash and soak urad dhal and rice for 15 minutes. Drain water completely and grind to a firm, coarse paste (sprinkle water if necessary). Mix in crushed pepper and required salt. Pour 3 tbsp of hot oil, mix evenly using fingertips to make a firm dough. Divide into marble sized balls. On a wet cloth, flatten the balls into very thin vadas using your fingers. Make a hole in the centre of each vada. Heat oil in a kadai. Deep fry a few vadas at a time. When half done, remove the vadas from the oil. Keep aside. Quickly prepare all the vadas in hot oil till half done. Finally deep fry the half done vadas till they become crispy and golden brown.

Note

This vada is supposed to be very auspicious and is prepared for the God Hanuman on festival days.

Aval Kola Vadai

(RICE FLAKES VADA)

Ingredients for 10 to 12 vadas

Rice flakes	*2 cups*
Grated coconut	*1 cup*
Ginger	*1" piece, finely chopped*
Green chillies	*8, finely chopped*
Coriander leaves	*a few, finely chopped*
Asafoetida	*a pinch*
Salt	*to taste*
Oil	*for deep frying*

Method

Crush the rice flakes, soak in water for 1-2 hours. Drain. Add coconut, ginger, green chillies, coriander leaves, asafoetida and required salt. Knead well using your hand. Divide into marble sized balls. Flatten into ½" thick vadas on a plastic sheet. Heat a dosa tawa. Arrange 5 or 6 vadas on the tawa. Pour a little oil around the vadas. Keep covered with a lid on a reduced flame. When the bottom is golden brown, turn over to the other side. Cook till both sides are crisp and serve.

Mysore Bonda

(LENTIL BALLS)

Ingredients for 10 balls

Whole urad dhal	*1 cup*
Rice	*1 tsp*
Green chillies	*2*
Coconut bits	*2 tsp*
Pepper corns	*1 tsp*
Curry leaves	*a few*
Salt	*to taste*
Oil	*for deep frying*

Method

Wash and soak urad dhal and rice for about 2 hours. Drain water and grind to a smooth, fluffy paste in grinder with green chillies, sprinkling required water.

Mysore Bonda

Add required salt, curry leaves, coconut pieces and pepper corns and mix well. Heat oil in a kadai. Divide the batter into small rough balls and deep fry till golden brown.

Vazakkai Vadai

(RAW BANANA VADA)

Ingredients for 10 to 12 vadas

Raw banana	*2, grated finely*
Rice flour	*2 tbsp*
Onion	*1*
Ginger	*1" piece*
Spinach	*1 small bunch, finely chopped*
Coriander leaves	*a few*
Curry leaves	*a few*
Salt	*to taste*
Oil	*for deep frying*

Method

Mix all the ingredients together to prepare a stiff dough. Prepare small vadas and deep fry till golden brown.

Methu Vadai

Methu Vadai

(SOFT VADAS)

Ingredients for 10 vadas

Whole urad dhal	*1 cup*
Rice	*1 tbsp*
Green chillies	*4*
Curry leaves	*a few*
Salt	*to taste*
Oil	*for deep frying*

Method

Wash and soak urad dhal and rice for about 2 hours. Drain water completely and add green chillies. Grind to a smooth fluffy batter. Do not add water, the batter should be stiff, otherwise vadas cannot be prepared in the right shape. Mix required salt and add curry leaves. Heat oil in a kadai. Divide the batter into small parts. Flatten each ball into a vada shape on a banana leaf or plastic sheet. Make a hole with your finger in the centre of each vada. Deep fry vadas in hot oil till golden brown.

Note

One tsp of pepper corns and 1 tsp of chopped coconut can be added to the batter to make the vadas tastier. Batter should be ground for at least 45 minutes and used immediately, otherwise the vadas consume more oil.

Pudalangai Vadai

(SNAKE GOURD VADA)

Ingredients for 10 vadas

Snake gourd	*500 gms, grated finely*
Fried gram	*4 tbsp*
Aniseed	*1 tsp*
Red chillies	*5 or 6*
Rice flour	*4 tbsp*
Onions	*2, finely chopped*
Coriander leaves	*a few, finely chopped*
Curry leaves	*a few, finely chopped*
Salt	*to taste*
Oil	*for deep frying*

Method

Dry roast aniseed and red chillies. Grind to a powder with fried gram and required salt. Sauté the snake gourd well in a little oil. Mix snake gourd, powdered ingredients and other ingredients to make a stiff dough. Heat oil in a kadai. Prepare these vadas on a plastic sheet and deep fry till golden brown.

Mangalore Bonda

Ingredients for 20 bondas

Rava	*1 cup*
Maida	*1 cup*
Rice flour	*1 cup*
Thick sour curd	*1 cup*
Onion	*1, finely chopped*
Green chillies	*4, finely chopped*
Coriander leaves	*1 tbsp, finely chopped*
Curry leaves	*2 tbsp, finely chopped*
Baking soda	*a pinch*
Salt	*to taste*
Oil	*for deep frying*

Method

Mix all the ingredients together in a bowl. Prepare stiff dough with a little water and keep it covered for about 5 to 6 hours. Divide the dough into small balls. Heat oil and deep fry the balls till golden brown. Serve hot with any chutney.

Note

Chopped greens can be mixed in the dough and palak bondas can be prepared.

Vazhakai Bajji

(DEEP FRIED RAW BANANA)

Ingredients

Raw banana	*1*
Channa dhal flour	*1 cup*
Rice flour	*½ cup*
Chilli powder	*1 tsp*
Turmeric powder	*½ tsp*
Salt	*to taste*
Oil	*for deep frying*

Method

Peel the banana and slice into thin, circular pieces. Mix channa dhal flour, rice flour, turmeric powder, chilli powder and required salt in a bowl. Add required water. Prepare thick batter. Dip each slice in the batter so that a thick coating is formed. Heat oil in a kadai and deep fry till golden brown. Serve with tomato ketchup or chutney.

Note

Similarly, potato, brinjal, snake gourd or onion can also be made into bajji.

Vazhakai Bajji

Kaikari Bonda

(VEGETABLE BONDA)

Ingredients for 10 to 12 bondas

Potatoes	*3*
Mustard seeds	*1 tsp*
Green chillies	*4, chopped*
Onion	*1, chopped*
Carrot and beans	*1 cup, finely chopped*
Peas	*½ cup*
Channa dhal flour	*1 cup*
Rice flour	*2 tsp*
Chilli powder	*1 tsp*
Salt	*to taste*
Oil	*for deep frying*

Method

Boil potatoes, peel and mash well. Heat oil in a kadai. Let mustard seeds splutter, add green chillies and onion. Sauté. Now add all the vegetables and cook in a little water for a few minutes. Add mashed potatoes, required salt and sauté together for a few minutes. Cool the mixture. Divide into small balls. Keep aside. Mix channa dhal flour, rice flour, chilli powder and required salt with water to prepare a batter as for bajji. Heat oil in a kadai. Dip each vegetable ball in the batter and deep fry to a golden brown colour.

Mundhiri Pakoda

(CASHEW PAKODA OR CASHEW NUT FRITTERS)

Ingredients

Whole cashew nuts	*50 gms*
Channa dhal flour	*¼ cup*
Maida	*1 tsp*
Rice flour	*2 tsp*
Chilli powder	*1 tsp*
Turmeric powder	*a pinch*
Salt	*to taste*
Oil	*for deep frying*

Method

Mix together all the ingredients except cashew nuts. Add 2 tbsp hot oil into the mixture. Mix the cashew nuts and sufficient water to prepare a stiff dough. Heat oil in a kadai. Deep fry little pieces of dough till golden brown (take care to see that each pakoda has at least one cashew nut).

Murungaikai Vadai

(DRUMSTICK VADA)

Ingredients for 10 vadas

Drumstick	*3*
Channa dhal	*1 cup*
Fried gram	*¾ cup*
Aniseeds	*1 tsp*
Onion	*3, finely chopped*
Green chillies	*8, finely chopped*
Garlic	*2 cloves, finely chopped*
Turmeric powder	*a pinch*
Salt	*to taste*
Oil	*for deep frying*

Method

Wash and soak channa dhal for 2 hours in water with fried gram. Cut drumsticks into 4 to 5 pieces. Add salt and turmeric powder and cook well. After cooling, take out the pulp, using a spoon. Keep aside. Drain the soaked dhals and grind with green chillies, onion, garlic and required salt. Mix aniseed and drumstick pulp and make a stiff dough. Heat oil in a kadai. Prepare small vadas on a plastic sheet and deep fry till golden brown.

Urulai Kizangu Bonda

(POTATO BONDA)

Ingredients

Potato	*6*
Green chillies	*3*
Chilli powder	*1 tsp*
Turmeric powder	*a pinch*
Garam masala	*1 tsp*
Mustard seeds	*1 tsp*
Lemon	*1*
Channa dhal flour	*½ cup*
Rice flour	*¼ cup*
Salt	*to taste*
Oil	*for deep frying*

Urulai Kizangu Bonda

Method

Boil potatoes, peel and mash well. Heat a little oil in a kadai. Let mustard seeds splutter. Fry green chillies. Mix garam masala and required salt. Add and sauté the mashed potatoes for a few minutes. After cooling, squeeze in a lemon. Mix well. Divide into small balls. Keep aside. Heat oil in a kadai. Mix channa dhal flour, rice flour, turmeric powder, chilli powder and required salt in a bowl. Add required water and prepare thick batter as for bajji. Dip each potato ball in the batter and deep fry to a golden brown colour.

Kuzhipaniyaram I

(SOFT RICE BALLS)

Ingredients for 10 to 15 paniyarams

Raw rice	*1 cup*
Parboiled rice	*½ cup*
Fenugreek seeds	*1 tsp*
Channa dhal	*2 tsp*
Urad dhal	*2 tsp*
Onion	*2*
Green chillies	*3*
Ginger	*1 inch piece, finely chopped*
Curry leaves	*a few*
Salt	*to taste*
Oil	*for deep frying*

Method

Wash and soak raw rice, parboiled rice and fenugreek for 3 hours. Grind together, add required salt and prepare a batter as for dosa. Heat a little oil in a kadai. Fry the dhals, then onion, ginger, green chillies and curry leaves and mix in the batter. In a kuzhiappa kadai, pour a little oil in each of the depressions. Then pour one ladle of batter in it and cook. When the bottom is cooked, turn over to the other side using a stick and cook both sides to a golden brown colour. Serve hot with any chutney.

Kuzhi Aappam/ Kuzhipaniyaram II

(SOFT RICE BALLS)

Ingredients for 10 to 12 aappams

Parboiled rice	*1½ cups*
Urad dhal	*½ cup*
Fenugreek seeds	*1 tsp*
Salt	*to taste*
Gingelly oil	*as required*
To season	
Mustard seeds	*1 tsp*
Channa dhal	*2 tsp*
Urad dhal	*2 tsp*
Green chillies	*2 to 3*
Ginger	*1" piece*
Curry leaves	*a few*

Method

Wash and soak dhal, rice and fenugreek for 3 hours. Grind together to a smooth batter like that for dosa. Mix in required salt and allow to ferment for 5 to 6 hours. Season with given seasonings and mix in the batter. Continue and prepare kuzhipaniyaram as in the previous recipe.

Note

If batter is used without fermenting, sour buttermilk can be added.

Vella Aappam

(SWEET SOFT RICE BALLS)

Ingredients for 10 to 12 aappams

Raw rice	*1 cup*
Powdered jaggery	*1 cup*
Ghee	*1 cup*
Cardamom	*3*
Coconut pieces	*1 tbsp*
Wheat flour	*1 tbsp*
Ripe banana	*½*

Method

Wash and soak rice for 2-3 hours, then grind to a smooth paste. Add jaggery and banana and grind together to make a thick batter. If required, mix wheat flour into the batter, without any lumps, to thicken it. Leave the batter for 4-5 hours. Add the coconut pieces and cardamom. Pour 1 tsp of ghee in the depressions of hot kuzhi appa kadai and then pour the batter into each depression. Cook both sides to a golden brown colour as in the previous recipe.

Karaadai

(STEAMED RICE VADA)

Ingredients for 10 to 12 vadas

Processed rice flour	*2 cups*
Dry black-eyed beans	*½ cup, soaked the previous day*
Green chillies	*4*
Ginger	*1 inch piece, finely chopped*
Curry leaves	*a few*
Salt	*to taste*
Butter	*as required*

Refer Crispy Snacks for preparation of processed rice flour.

Method

In a kadai dry roast the rice flour to a light pinkish colour. In a bowl mix the rice flour, add beans, chillies, ginger, curry leaves and required salt. Add a little water and prepare a stiff dough. Divide into small balls and flatten into thin vadas on a plastic sheet. Poke a hole in the centre of vadas. Steam cook in idli cooker for 10 minutes till done. Serve with butter. This is specially prepared on the day of Vratha (fast) called Nonbu.

Vella Karaadai

(STEAMED SWEET RICE VADA)

Ingredients

Processed rice flour	*2 cups*
Powdered jaggery	*1½ cups*
Cardamom powder	*1 tsp*

Refer crispy snacks for preparation of processed rice flour.

Method

In a kadai dry roast the rice flour to a mild pinkish colour. Mix the jaggery, rice flour, cardamom powder and prepare a stiff dough adding required water. Divide into small balls and flatten into thin vadas on a plastic sheet. Poke a hole in the centre of vadas. Steam cook in idli cooker for 15 to 20 minutes till done. Serve with butter. This is also specially prepared on the Vratha day called Nonbu.

Venkaya Pakoda or Thool Pakoda

(CRISPY ONION FRITTERS)

Ingredients

Channa dhal flour	*1 cup*
Rice flour	*2 cups*
Onion	*4, finely chopped*
Green chillies	*6, finely chopped*
Coriander leaves	*a few, finely chopped*
Salt	*to taste*
Oil	*for deep frying*

Method

Mix all the ingredients together in a large bowl. Heat oil in a kadai. Pour 2 tbsp of hot oil in the bowl and prepare a stiff, semi-dry dough (sprinkling required water). Drop the dough, in pieces, in the hot oil and deep fry till golden brown.

Venkaya Pakoda or Thool Pakoda

Kothukadalai Sundal

Methu Pakoda

(SOFT FRITTERS)

Ingredients

Channa dhal flour	*1 cup*
Rice flour	*1 cup*
Onion	*1, finely chopped*
Green chillies	*5, finely chopped*
Ginger	*1" piece, finely chopped*
Curry leaves	*a few, finely chopped*
Coriander leaves	*a few finely chopped*
Coriander seeds	*1 tsp*
Cooking soda	*1 tsp*
Ghee or vanaspathi	*3 tsp*
Salt	*to taste*
Oil	*for deep frying*

Method

In a bowl, mix cooking soda and vanaspathi together till frothy. Then add all other ingredients and mix with a little water to prepare a stiff dough. Heat oil in a kadai. Divide the dough into small rough balls and deep fry till golden brown.

Kothukadalai Sundal

(CHANNA DRY FRY)

Ingredients

Kabuli channa or	
black channa	*1 cup*
Red chillies	*3*
Mustard seeds	*1 tsp*
Curry leaves	*a few*
Grated coconut	*2 tbsp, optional*
Salt	*as required*
Oil	*for seasoning*

Method

Wash and soak channa overnight. Pressure cook (with just enough water) with a little salt. Heat 1 tsp of oil in a kadai. Season with the mustard seeds, red chillies and curry leaves. Then add cooked channa along with the water. Shallow fry for a few minutes till all the moisture is absorbed. Decorate with grated coconut.

Thengai Mangai Pattani Sundal

(PEAS DRY FRY WITH MANGO)

Ingredients

Dry white peas or	
green peas	*1 cup*
Green chillies	*3*
Mustard seeds	*½ tsp*
Curry leaves	*a few*
Raw mango	*2 tbsp, chopped*
Grated coconut	*1 tbsp*
Sambar powder	*1 tsp*
Salt	*as required*
Oil	*for seasoning*
Lemon juice	*1 tsp*

Method

Wash and soak peas overnight. Pressure cook with just enough water and required salt for up to 1 whistle only as peas cook fast. Heat a little oil in a kadai. Allow mustard seeds to splutter and fry chillies and curry leaves. Then add cooked peas with the used water. Add a little sambar powder; shallow fry for a few minutes till moisture is absorbed. Decorate with chopped raw mango and grated coconut. Squeeze a little lemon juice on top and serve.

Note

Any dry legume can be prepared in the same way as sundal, e.g., rajma, black-eyed beans, broad beans etc. Split channa dhal or moong dhal can also be used.

GRAVIES

Gravies are an essential part of south Indian meals. They usually accompany cooked rice to give the desired taste and spiciness to the meal.

Either fresh or dry vegetables are cooked in a specific base to form the gravy. The base varies according to availability of ingredients in a particular region. Common bases are tamarind, buttermilk, coconut and dhal, with some variations among the four states of south India. In Kerala, a lot of coconut, coconut milk and buttermilk are used and for seasoning, coconut oil is used. Andhrites use more tamarind and chillies, so the gravies are very spicy. A lot of ghee is used to reduce the spiciness. In Karnataka, most of the gravies are slightly sweetish to taste, as jaggery or sugar (in small quantities) is often mixed in the base. Refined groundnut oil is used for seasoning. In Tamil Nadu, the gravies are much less spicy and milder than Andhra and gingelly oil is used for seasoning.

There are a few standard gravies prepared as part of most meals in the southern states. The most popular is called sambar in Tamil Nadu, pulusu in Andhra and Karnataka and kootan in Kerala. This is prepared with a tamarind base, either with or without lentils (dhal). Another common gravy is rasam (Tamil Nadu) also known as chaaru in other states. This is a diluted gravy prepared with or without dhal. This is also served as a strongly flavoured appetiser. It is very good for recovering patients and children.

Another well known gravy is kootu. This consists mainly of vegetables and a thick base made out of coconut and dhal. Kootu is not as spicy as sambar.

Sambar Powder

For 1 kg

Good quality red chillies	*250 gms*
Coriander seeds	*500 gms*
Channa dhal	*100 gms*
Toor dhal	*100 gms*
Whole turmeric	*100 gms*
Pepper corns	*50 gms*
Jeera	*50 gms*

Method

Dry all the ingredients in the sun or dry roast in a hot kadai and pound in a flour mill into a smooth powder. Store in an airtight container.

Rasa Powder

(USED FOR RASAM)

For 1 kg

Good quality red chillies	*100 gms*
Coriander seeds	*500 gms*
Channa dhal	*100 gms*
Toor dhal	*100 gms*
Turmeric	*100 gms*
Pepper corns	*100 gms*
Jeera	*100 gms*
Dry curry leaves1 cup	

Method

Dry all the ingredients in the sun or dry roast in a hot kadai and pound in a flour mill into a smooth powder. Store in an airtight container.

Sambar

(DHAL AND TAMARIND GRAVY)

Ingredients

Tamarind	*Large, lemon-sized amount*
Toor dhal	*1 cup*
Sambar powder	*4 tsp*
Any one vegetable like brinjal, ladies finger, radish, broad beans, potato, etc.	*250 gms, cut into pieces*
or	
Drumstick	*3, cut into 3″ pieces*
or	
Small onions	*250 gms, peeled*
Salt	*to taste*
Oil	*as required*
To season	
Mustard seeds	*½ tsp*
Fenugreek seeds	*½ tsp*
Red chilli	*1*
Green chilli	*1*
Chopped coriander leaves	*to decorate*

Method

Pressure cook toor dhal, with a little turmeric powder. Keep aside. Extract tamarind juice in 3 cups of water. Add sambar powder, required salt and boil for 5 minutes. Add the vegetables and boil till the vegetables are cooked. Add cooked dhal and required water. Boil for a few minutes. Season and decorate.

Sambar

More Sambar

(BUTTERMILK SAMBAR)

Ingredients

Butter milk	*2 cups*
Toor dhal	*½ cup*
Coriander seeds	*2 tsp*
Channa dhal	*1 tsp*
Pepper	*½ tsp*
Red chillies	*4*
Fenugreek seeds	*½ tsp*
Turmeric powder	*a pinch*
Drumstick	*2*
Salt	*to taste*
Oil	*as required*

To season

Mustard seeds, curry leaves

Method

Pressure cook, toor dhal. Keep aside. Cut the drumstick into 2" pieces, cook with a little turmeric powder and required salt. Keep aside. Fry and grind together coriander seeds, channa dhal, pepper, red chillies, fenugreek seeds into a paste. Mix the cooked dhal and the ground paste with water. Add the drumstick pieces. Boil for a few minutes with required salt. Pour in thick buttermilk and bring to one boil. Remove from fire. Season.

Hotel Sambar

Ingredients

Small onion	*200 gms, peeled*
Tomato	*2, cut*
Tamarind	*small lemon-sized amount*
Toor dhal	*½ cup*
Green chillies	*3*
Sugar or jaggery	*1 tsp*
Turmeric powder	*a pinch*
Salt	*to taste*
Oil	*as required*

For masala, roast in a little oil and grind to powder

Channa dhal	*1 tsp*
Coriander seeds	*3 tsp*
Red chillies	*4*
Asafoetida	*a pinch*
Poppy seeds	*1 tsp*
Jeera	*½ tsp*
Pepper	*½ tsp*

To season

Mustard seeds	*1 tsp*
Red chillies	*2*
Curry leaves	*a few*
Chopped coriander leaves	*to decorate*

Method

Pressure cook toor dhal. Keep aside. Shallow fry onions with tomato and green chillies. Extract tamarind in 3 cups of water. Boil the fried onions in this, till done. Add turmeric powder, required salt, and ground masala spices and boil for a few more minutes. Now mix the cooked toor dhal and sugar. Boil for a few minutes.

Note

Hotel sambar should be very diluted. It is a good accompaniment for idli, dosa, adai, uppuma etc.

Arachivitta Sambar

(SAMBAR WITH FRESHLY GROUND SPICES)

Ingredients

Toor dhal	*¾ cup*
Tamarind	*large lemon-sized amount*
Turmeric powder	*a pinch*
Coriander seeds	*6 tsp*
Red chillies	*6*
Channa dhal	*2 tsp*
Fenugreek seeds	*½ tsp*
Grated coconut	*2 tbsp*
White radish	*250 gms*
Salt	*to taste*

Oil	*as required*
To season	
Mustard seeds, asafoetida	
Coriander leaves to decorate	

Method

Pressure cook toor dhal with turmeric powder. Fry and grind coriander seeds, red chillies, fenugreek seeds, channa dhal and grated coconut into a smooth paste. Extract juice from tamarind. In a vessel, cook radish with required salt and turmeric powder. Add tamarind extract to this and boil for 2 minutes. Add ground paste and dhal and boil well. Season. Decorate with coriander leaves.

Note

Red radish, sambar onions, drumstick or white pumpkin can also be used.

Keerai Sambar

(GREEN LEAVES SAMBAR)

Ingredients

Any variety of greens	*1 bunch*
Tamarind	*medium lemon-sized amount*
Toor dhal	*1 cup*
Green chilli	*1*
Turmeric powder	*a pinch*
Salt	*to taste*
To grind	
Coriander seeds	*3 tbsp*
Channa dhal	*1 tsp*
Fenugreek seeds	*½ tsp*
Red chillies	*5*
Asafoetida	*a pinch*
Oil	*as required*
To season	
Mustard seeds	*1 tsp*
Peanuts	*1 tsp*

Method

Pressure cook toor dhal with a pinch of turmeric powder. In a kadai, fry the ingredients for grinding and powder in mixie. Keep aside. Extract tamarind juice by soaking it in 2 cups of water. Wash the greens after removing the roots, drain and chop finely. Sauté in 1 tsp of oil in a kadai with a green chilli. When the moisture dries up add to the tamarind extract and boil together. Add the ground powder and required salt. Boil for 5 minutes. Finally, add the cooked toor dhal. Boil together and season.

Brinjal Rasa Vangi

(SAMBAR WITH SEASONINGS)

Ingredients

Brinjals	*500 gms, cut into pieces*
Toor dhal	*½ cup*
Tamarind	*small lemon-sized amount*
Turmeric powder	*a pinch*
Mustard seeds	*1 tsp*
Green chillies	*2*
Red chillies	*3*
Curry leaves	*a few*
Salt	*to taste*
Oil	*as required*

Method

Pressure cook toor dhal and keep aside. Extract 1 cup of tamarind juice. Cook brinjals in tamarind extract with turmeric powder and required salt. Add the cooked toor dhal and boil for a few minutes. Season with mustard seeds, green chillies, red chillies and curry leaves.

Sempangi Pitlai (Karnataka)

Kathirikkai Pitlai

(BRINJAL GRAVY WITH TAMARIND AND COCONUT)

Ingredients

Toor dhal	*½ cup*
Turmeric powder	*a pinch*
Black channa/black eyed beans/soaked previously	
or	
Whole peanuts	*½ cup*
Brinjal	*250 gms*
Pappads	*4*
Tamarind	*Medium lemon-sized amount*
Salt	*to taste*
Oil	*as required*
To grind	
Channa dhal	*1 tsp*
Coriander seeds	*2 tsp*
Red chillies	*6*
Grated coconut	*½ cup*
To season	

Mustard seeds, curry leaves, fenugreek seeds, asafoetida.

Method

Pressure cook toor dhal with a little turmeric powder. Keep aside. Separately cook channa/kidney beans/peanuts with required salt. Keep aside. In a little oil, fry coriander seeds, channa dhal, red chillies, finally add coconut before putting off the flame. Grind to a powder in the mixie. Extract tamarind juice after soaking it in 2 cups of water and boil with required salt. Clean and slit the brinjal into 4. Add the cut brinjal, cooked channa, required salt, etc. to the tamarind extract and boil till done. Add the ground powder and boil again for a few minutes. Now add the cooked toor dhal and bring to a boil. Add given seasonings. Lastly deep fry the pappads and add into the pitla when it is still hot.

Note

Instead of brinjal, bitter gourd may be used.

Sempangi Pitlai (Karnataka)

(VEGETABLE GRAVY WITH TAMARIND AND COCONUT)

Ingredients

Toor dhal	*1 cup*
Tamarind	*large lemon-sized amount*
Potatoes, chow-chow, broad beans, brinjals	*1 cup each, cut into pieces*
Drumstick, greens stem	*1 cup, cut into 3″ pieces*
Turmeric powder	*a pinch*
Rice flour	*½ tsp*
Salt	*to taste*
Oil	*as required*
To grind	
Red chillies	*4*
Urad dhal	*1 tsp*
Pepper	*5 or 6*
Grated coconut	*1 tsp*
Coriander seeds	*1 tsp, optional*
To season	
Mustard seeds	*½ tsp*
Channa dhal	*½ tsp*
Asafoetida	*a pinch*
Curry leaves	*a few*

Method

Pressure cook toor dhal. Keep aside. Extract tamarind in 2 cups of water. Cook the vegetables with required salt and turmeric powder in the tamarind extract. Fry the ingredients for grinding and grind to a powder. Add this powder and cooked dhal to the vegetables, boil for a few minutes and season. If the gravy needs thickening, add rice flour paste and boil for 5 seconds.

More Kuzhambu

(BUTTERMILK GRAVY)

Ingredients

Thick buttermilk	*3 cups*
Coriander seeds	*2 tsp*
Toor dhal	*1 tsp*
Jeera	*½ tsp*
Rice	*½ tsp*
Grated coconut	*½ cup*
Green chillies	*3*
White pumpkin	*1 slice*
Turmeric powder	*½ tsp*
Salt	*to taste*
Coconut oil	*as required*

To season

Mustard seeds, curry leaves

Method

Cook white pumpkin separately in a little water with turmeric powder and required salt. Soak coriander seeds, toor dhal, jeera and rice for 10 minutes. Grind the soaked ingredients, grated coconut and green chillies with a little buttermilk to a smooth paste. Dissolve the ground paste in thick buttermilk, add required salt and cooked pumpkin and bring to boil. Switch off the flame and season.

Note

Instead of pumpkin, ladies finger, chow-chow or colocasia can be used.

More Charu/ Pachai More Kuzhambu/ Thalithukottina More Kuzhambu

(SEASONED BUTTERMILK)

Ingredients

Sour buttermilk	*2 cups*
Rice flour	*1 tsp*
Mustard seeds	*½ tsp*
Urad dhal	*1 tsp*
Tymol seeds	*½ tsp*
Fenugreek seeds	*½ tsp*
Green chillies	*3, slit*
Curry leaves	*a few*
Salt	*to taste*
Gingelly oil	*as required*

Method

Mix rice flour and salt in buttermilk. In a kadai, fry mustard seeds, urad dhal, tymol seeds, fenugreek seeds and green chillies. Pour the buttermilk mixture and add a few curry leaves, bring to boil and put off the flame.

Vatha Kuzhambu

(SPICY TAMARIND GRAVY)

Ingredients

Tamarind	*large lemon sized amount*
Red chillies	*6*
Toor dhal	*1 tsp*
Channa dhal	*1 tsp*
Mustard seeds	*½ tsp*
Asafoetida	*a little*
Curry leaves	*a few*
Sambar powder	*4 tsp*
Manothakkal vattral (dried black nightshade) or Sundaikaivattral (dried bitter berries)	*¼ cup*
Salt	*to taste*
Gingelly oil	*as required*

Method

Extract tamarind in 3 cups of water. Heat oil in a deep pan, season with mustard seeds, asafoetida and curry leaves. Add and fry red chillies, and the dhals. To this add and fry the dried vegetables (vattral) well. Add and fry the sambar powder for just 5 seconds. Immediately add the tamarind extract and required salt. Allow to boil for 15-20 minutes. A little rice flour paste may be added to make the kuzhambu thick.

Note
Any desired vegetables like brinjals, ladies finger, cluster beans and broad beans can also be used.

Kottu Kuzhambu

(SPICY TAMARIND GRAVY WITH FRESH VEGETABLES)

Method
The vatha kuzhambu as in the previous recipe is prepared with fresh vegetables like broad beans, brinjal, ladies finger and small onions. The vegetables are added with tamarind extract and salt before boiling.

Venthiya Kuzhambu

(SPICY TAMARIND GRAVY WITH FENUGREEK SEEDS)

Method
Vatha kuzhambu as in previous recipe is prepared without any dry or fresh vegetables. 1 tsp of fenugreek seeds is also fried together with other ingredients.

Arai Puli Kuzhambu

(SPICY TAMARIND GRAVY WITH YAM AND COCONUT)

Method
In the same vatha kuzhambu, when frying other ingredients a few coconut pieces and 100 gms of elephant yam pieces are added.

Vada Kuzhambu

(DHAL VADA GRAVY)

Ingredients

Toor dhal	*½ cup*
Kabuli channa	*½ cup*
Black-eyed kidney beans	*½ cup*
Garlic	*4 flakes*
Aniseeds	*½ tsp*
Red chillies	*4*
Green chillies	*4*
Onion	*1 cup, finely chopped*
Tomato	*½ cup, finely chopped*
Chilli powder	*1 tsp*
Coriander powder	*1 tsp*
Jeera powder	*1 tsp*
Turmeric powder	*1 tsp*
Salt	*to taste*
Oil	*as required*
To season	
Mustard seeds	*1 tsp*
Cloves	*2*
Cinnamon	*1 small piece*
Aniseed	*½ tsp*
Cardamom	*2*
Bay leaves	*a few*
Curry leaves	*a few*

Method
Soak toor dhal, kabuli channa and black-eyed kidney beans for 23 hours. Grind with garlic, aniseeds, red chillies, green chillies, and required salt to a coarse paste without adding water. Spread on idli plates and steam cook in the idli cooker for 15-20 minutes. When done, cool the paste to room temperature and break into small pieces. Keep aside. In a kadai, add 4 tsp of oil. Fry given seasonings. Add and fry onion and then tomato. Add all the four powders and required salt and fry. Add half cup water. Boil till the raw flavour is removed. Mix the cooked dhal paste and sauté together for a few minutes. This goes well with idiappam, aappam, idli, dosai and poori.

Vadakari

(DHAL GRAVY)

Method

Only toor dhal and channa dhal in equal measures are used in this recipe instead of the 3 dhals given in previous one. The method is the same as for the vada kuzhambu recipe.

Vendaikai Race Kuzhambu

(LADIES FINGER GRAVY IN TAMARIND)

Ingredients

Tamarind	*small lemon-sized amount*
Ladies finger	*200 gms*
Green chillies	*5 or 6*
Salt	*to taste*
Gingelly oil	*as required*
To grind	
Fenugreek seeds	*½ tsp*
Rice	*½ tsp*
Channa dhal	*1 tsp*
Moong dhal	*1 tsp*
Toor dhal	*1 tsp*
Urad dhal	*1 tsp*
Coriander seeds	*2 tsp*
Red chillies	*6*
Pepper	*6 or 8*
To season	

Asafoetida, mustard seeds, curry leaves

Method

Dry roast fenugreek seeds and grind to a powder. In a little oil fry the ingredients for grinding separately and powder nicely. Cut each ladies finger into 2" pieces. In a kadai, heat oil, sauté green chillies and ladies finger. Extract tamarind juice in 2 cups of water and add into the kadai. Mix salt and all the ground powders. Boil till the vegetables is done and season.

Note

If brinjal or drumstick is used, it need not be sautéed.

Vendaikai Race Kuzhambu

Masala Kuzhambu

(MASALA GRAVY WITH CHANNA DHAL BALLS)

For kuzhambu

Tamarind	*medium lemon-sized amount*
Small onions	*½ cup*
Salt	*to taste*
Oil	*as required*

Fry and grind into a smooth paste (I)

Red chillies	*6*
Coriander seeds	*1 tbsp*
Channa dhal	*1 tsp*
Urad dhal	*1 tsp*
Pepper	*6*

Fry and grind into a smooth paste (II)

Cloves	*10*
Anise	*1 tsp*
Cardamom	*10*
Cinnamon	*2 pieces*
Poppy seeds	*2 tsp*

To season

Mustard seeds	*1 tsp*
Asafoetida	*a pinch*
Cloves	*2*
Curry leaves	*a few*
Anise	*½ tsp*
Oil	*little*

To prepare kuzhambu

Extract tamarind in 4 cups of water. Peel and chop the onions and sauté in a little oil. To the tamarind extract, add and mix spices paste I, 2/3rds of spices paste II, onion and required salt. Boil till the gravy is reduced to 2/3rds of its original amount. Fry the seasonings and add to gravy. Lastly, add the prepared bondas and put off the flame.

To prepare bondas

Channa dhal flour	*1 cup*
Rice flour	*½ cup*
Chilli powder	*1 tsp*
Spices paste II	*1/3rd*
Small onions	*½ cup, peeled and chopped*
Cooking soda	*a pinch*
Salt	*to taste*
Oil	*as required*

Masala Kuzhambu

Method

Mix these ingredients well with a little water until a thick batter is formed. Heat oil in a kadai. Drop the batter little by little into the oil with a spoon. Deep fry till golden brown. Keep aside.

Paruppu Urundai Kuzhambu

(TAMARIND GRAVY WITH LENTIL BALLS)

For parappu urundai

Toor dhal	*1 cup*
Red chillies	*8-9*
Asafoetida	*a pinch*
Mustard seeds	*1 tsp*
Green chillies	*2, chopped*
Onion	*½ cup, chopped*
Coconut grated	*½ cup, optional*
Rice flour	*1 tsp*
Salt	*to taste*
Oil	*as required*

Method

Clean and soak dhal in water for 1½ to 2 hours. Drain and grind dhal with red chillies, asafoetida and required salt, into a coarse firm paste. Heat a little oil in a pan, add mustard seeds and fry till they splutter. Add and fry green chillies and onions. Add the ground dhal paste, and stir till it changes its colour. When it is well-cooked, remove from fire. Add grated coconut and rice flour. Mix well. Make into small balls and keep aside.

For kuzhambu

Tamarind extract	*2 cups*
Red chillies	*6*
Toor dhal	*1 tsp*
Channa dhal	*1 tsp*
Fenugreek seeds	*½ tsp*
Mustard seeds	*½ tsp*
Asafoetida	*a pinch*
Curry leaves	*a few*
Sambar powder	*4 tsp*
Salt	*to taste*
Gingelly oil	*as required*

Method

Heat oil in a deep pan, season with mustard seeds, asafoetida and curry leaves. Add and fry red chillies, fenugreek seeds and the dhals. In the same, fry the sambar powder for just 5 seconds. Immediately add the tamarind extract and required salt. Allow to boil for 15-20 minutes.

For paruppu urundai kuzhambu

When the gravy is boiling drop two balls at a time, slowly. When the balls are cooked they will float to the top. Now add two more balls, wait till they float to the top. Similarly drop all the balls into the gravy and boil together for a few minutes.

Note

1 cup dhal gives approximately 10 balls.

If paruppu urundai kuzhambu is to be used after 4-5 hours the balls should not be kept in the gravy as they may break.

Paruppu Urundai More Kuzhambu

(LENTIL BALLS IN BUTTERMILK)

Method

Lentil balls are prepared as in the previous recipe and added to more kuzhambu as prepared in the paruppu urundai kuzhambu recipe.

Pakoda Kurma (Andhra)

(PAKODA MASALA GRAVY)

Ingredients

Cloves	*2*
Cardamoms	*2*
Cinnamon	*1" piece*
Curry leaves	*a few*
Onions	*2, sliced*
Turmeric powder	*½ tsp*
Chilli powder	*1 tsp*
Coriander powder	*1 tsp*
Tomatoes	*2, chopped*
Lemon juice	*1 tsp*

Salt	*to taste*
Oil	*as required*
To grind	
Grated coconut	*¼ cup*
Poppy seeds	*2 tsp*
To season	
Cashew nuts	*1 tsp*
Coriander leaves	*a few, chopped*

To prepare pakodas

Channa dhal	*2 cups, soaked for 2 hours*
Onions	*6, finely chopped*
Ginger-garlic paste	*½ tsp*
Curd	*1 tsp*
Salt	*to taste*
Oil	*for deep drying*

Drain and grind dhal to a coarse paste without using water. Add the rest of the ingredients and required salt. Roll into small balls. Deep fry. Keep aside.

To prepare kurma

In a heavy-bottomed vessel heat a little oil. Shallow fry cloves, cardamoms, curry leaves and onions. Add turmeric, chilli and coriander powders and sauté for a minute. Add tomatoes and shallow fry. Add the ground paste, required salt and required water. Let it simmer on a low flame. Gently add the prepared pakodas to the gravy and cook for 5 minutes. Put the flame off. Mix in lemon juice and season. Serve hot with rice.

Dhaniya Kuzhambu

(CORIANDER SEEDS GRAVY)

Ingredients

Tamarind	*small lemon-sized amount*
Coriander seeds	*¼ cup*
Red chillies	*3*
Pepper	*1 tsp*
Asafoetida	*a pinch*
Mustard seeds	*a little*
Curry leaves	*a few*
Salt	*to taste*
Gingelly oil	*as required*

Method

Fry and grind coriander seeds, red chillies, pepper, together with a little water to a smooth paste. Dissolve the paste in 2 cups of tamarind extract. In a kadai, heat 4 tsp of oil and fry mustard seeds and a few curry leaves. Pour the mixture in the kadai. Add salt. Boil until reduced to half.

Kalan (Kerala)

(VEGETABLES IN BUTTERMILK GRAVY)

Ingredients

Elephant yam	*300 gms*
Raw banana	*2, cut into long pieces*
Mildly sour thick buttermilk	*4 cups*
Green chillies	*6*
Pepper	*1 tsp*
Turmeric powder	*a pinch*
Grated coconut	*1 cup*
Salt	*to taste*
To season	
Mustard seeds	*1 tsp*
Red chillies	*2*
Curry leaves	*a few*
Coconut oil	*1 tsp*

Method

Grind coconut, pepper and green chillies to a smooth paste. Keep aside. Cook the vegetables in a little water together with required salt and turmeric powder. When the vegetables are half done, add buttermilk and boil. A layer of cream will form on top. Remove it. Keep aside. Keep removing the cream as and when it forms. Reduce the gravy to half its measure. Remove from fire. Mix in the prepared cream, coconut paste and required salt. Mix well and season.

Olan (Kerala)

Eriseri (Kerala)

(YAM AND BANANA IN COCONUT)

Ingredients

Elephant yam	*300 gms, cut into cubes*
Raw banana	*2, cut into cubes*
Coconut	*1 cup, grated*
Rice	*1 tsp*
Pepper	*1 tsp*
Turmeric powder	*1 tsp*
Salt	*to taste*
Coconut oil	*as required*

To season

Mustard seeds, curry leaves

Method

Cook the yam with turmeric powder and required salt. When half done, add bananas and cook. Grind together half cup coconut, pepper and rice. Add the ground paste to the cooked vegetables and boil together for a few minutes. Fry the remaining coconut to a golden colour in a little oil and add to the gravy. Boil well till the raw smell is removed and season.

Note

Cluster beans, snake gourd and pumpkin may also be used.

Olan (Kerala)

(PUMPKIN IN ITS OWN GRAVY)

Ingredients

Pumpkin	*400 gms, cut into pieces*
Green chillies	*4*
Curry leaves	*a few*
Salt	*to taste*
Coconut oil	*3 tsp*

Method

Cover and boil the pumpkin in 1 cup of water with required salt and slit green chillies. When it is cooking, mash the pumpkin a little, with a wooden ladle. Add raw coconut oil and curry leaves and mix well. Allow to cook in the water released by the pumpkin.

Note

This is a watery gravy and good for those with a weak digestive system.

Karugepillai Kuzhambu/ Milagu Kuzhambu

(PEPPER AND CURRY LEAVES GRAVY IN TAMARIND)

Ingredients

Fresh curry leaves	*2 cups*
Pepper	*1½ tsp*
Jeera	*½ tsp*
Red chillies	*6*
Tamarind	*small lemon-sized amount*
Salt	*to taste*
Gingelly oil	*as required*

To season

Mustard seeds, urad dhal

Method

Squeeze out thick tamarind extract. Grind all the ingredients, in the given order, to a smooth paste using water as required. Add required salt and dissolve the paste in tamarind extract. In a kadai, fry the mustard seeds and urad dhal in 2 tsp of gingelly oil for seasoning. Pour the ground paste into the kadai and allow to boil till it is reduced to half its quantity.

Note

This kuzhambu can be used for 3-4 days.

Alternative method

Grind all the ingredients together, including tamarind to a smooth paste, sprinkling water if required. Mix the required salt. In a kadai, fry mustard seeds and urad dhal for seasoning. Add the ground paste and sauté for a few minutes till the moisture is fully absorbed.

The quantity of curry leaves and pepper can be increased or decreased according to the requirement.

Thengai Masala Kuzhambu

(MASALA GRAVY WITH COCONUT)

Ingredients

Tamarind	*small lemon-sized amount*
Small onions	*10, peeled*
Tender brinjals	*250 gms*
Salt	*to taste*
Gingelly oil	*as required*
To grind	
Cloves	*6*
Cardamom	*6*
Poppy seeds	*1 tsp*
Cinnamon	*½" piece*
Channa dhal	*2 tsp*
Coriander seeds	*4 tsp*
Red chillies	*8*
Coconut	*1 cup, grated*
To season	
Mustard seeds	*1 tsp*
Asafoetida	*a few*
Channa dhal	*1 tsp*
Fenugreek seeds	*½ tsp*

Method

In a little oil, fry all the given ingredients for grinding in the order listed above. Grind to a smooth paste. Keep aside. Extract 2 cups of tamarind juice. In a heavy-bottomed vessel, heat oil. Lightly fry all the seasonings. Add the onions and sauté. Add the brinjals. Pour in the tamarind extract. Boil well till brinjals are done. Add required salt and ground paste. Boil together for a few minutes.

Mangottai Kuzhambu

(TAMARIND GRAVY WITH MANGO SEEDS)

Ingredients

Salted and dried mango	*2*
Tamarind	*medium lemon-sized amount*
Rice four	*1 tsp*
Coriander seeds	*1 tsp*
Pepper	*5*
Red chillies	*4*
Jeera	*1 tsp*
Salt	*to taste*
Oil	*as required*
To season	
Mustard seeds	*1 tsp*
Asafoetida	*a pinch*
Curry leaves	*a few*

Method

Fry red chillies, coriander seeds, pepper, jeera. Remove the seeds from the dried mango. Grind the fried ingredients and mango seeds together. Keep aside. Cut the dry mangos into small pieces and cook in a little water. Extract tamarind in 2 cups of water and boil. Add the mango pieces and mix the ground paste, and if required, salt, and boil. Mix in a little rice flour paste for thickness, and season.

Note
This is good for people with weak stomachs.

Mangai Kuzhambu (Karnataka)

(TAMARIND GRAVY WITH RAW MANGO)

Ingredients

Tamarind	*very small lemon-sized amount*
Sour raw mangos	*4, cut into pieces*
Jaggery	*small piece*
Rice flour	*1 tsp*
Salt	*to taste*
Gingelly oil	*as required*
To grind	
Fry and grind into a smooth paste	
Coriander seeds	*2 tbsp*
Fenugreek seeds	*1 tsp*

Red chillies	*5*
Asafoetida	*a pinch*
To season	
Mustard seeds, curry leaves	

Method

Extract tamarind in 2 cups of water. Add mango pieces and mix with ground paste and required salt. Boil till the mango is done. Add jaggery and season. If required, add a little rice flour paste to thicken the gravy.

Keerai Masiyal

(MASHED GREENS GRAVY)

Ingredients

Any variety of greens	*1 bunch*
Jeera	*1 tsp*
Salt	*to taste*
To season	
Mustard seeds	*1 tsp*
Urad dhal	*1 tsp*
Jeera	*½ tsp*
Red chillies	*2*
Coconut oil	*a little*

Method

Clean and cut the greens. Cook with just enough water, jeera and required salt. Cool and mash the greens. Fry mustard seeds, urad dhal, jeera and red chillies in coconut oil, add to the mashed greens and boil together for 2 minutes.

Keerai Puli

(COOKED GREENS IN TAMARIND)

Any variety of greens	*1 bunch, chopped very finely*
Tamarind	*a little*
Green chillies	*2*
Jeera	*½ tsp*
Grated coconut	*½ cup*
Salt	*to taste*
Oil	*as required*
To season	
Mustard seeds	*½ tsp*
Asafoetida	*a pinch*
Red chilli	*1*

Method

Extract tamarind in 1 cup of water. Cook greens in the tamarind extract with required salt and green chillies. Grind coconut, jeera into a smooth paste and add to the greens. Boil well and season.

Keerai Puli

Chenai Masiyal

(MASHED YAM GRAVY)

Ingredients

Small yam, elephant yam	*500 gms*
Mustard seeds	*½ tsp*
Urad dhal	*½ tsp*
Channa dhal	*½ tsp*
Ginger	*1 piece, grated*
Red chillies	*2*
Green chillies	*2*
Turmeric powder	*½ tsp*
Curry leaves	*a few*
Roasted fenugreek powder	*½ tsp*
Asafoetida	*a pinch*
Salt	*to taste*
Gingelly oil	*as required*
Lemon	*1*

Method

Peel and cut yam into big pieces and pressure cook with required salt. Cool to room temperature and blend in the mixie to a coarse paste. Keep aside. Heat gingelly oil in a kadai. Fry mustard seeds, urad dhal, channa dhal, ginger, red chillies, green chillies, turmeric powder, curry leaves and asafoetida. Now pour the mashed yam, add required salt, fenugreek powder and a little water. Boil for a few minutes till the gravy becomes thick. Squeeze juice of one lemon when cooled.

Note

The same recipe may also be prepared with tamarind. In this case, the vegetables should be cooked in tamarind extract.

Avial

(VEGETABLE IN COCONUT AND CURD)

Ingredients

Potato	*3*
Elephant yam	*100 gms*
Raw banana	*1*
Broad beans	*50 gms*
Carrot and beans	*100 gms*
Ash gourd	*1 piece*
Chow-chow	*1*
Drumstick	*2*
Grated coconut	*1 cup*
Green chillies	*6*
Jeera	*1 tsp*
Rice	*1 tsp*
Fresh thick curd	*1½ cup*
Curry leaves	*a few*
Turmeric powder	*a pinch*
Salt	*to taste*
Coconut oil	*as required*

Method

Peel yam, chow-chow, ash gourd, potatoes and raw banana. Cut all the vegetables into big pieces. Cook all the vegetables with turmeric powder and required salt. Grind together grated coconut, green chillies, jeera and rice. A little curd may be added if required. Add this paste to the cooked vegetables and boil. After cooling, mix whipped curd and serve. Season with curry leaves in coconut oil.

Note

This is a good accompaniment to adai and dhal rice.

Avial

Ezhukari

Ezhukari

(GRAVY WITH 7 VEGETABLES)

Ingredients

Chow-chow, sweet potato, raw banana, elephant yam, brinjal, colacasia, potatoes, broad beans, fresh beans seeds (mochai)	*Any combination of 7 to 8 vegetables totalling ½ kg approx. may be used*
Toor dhal	*1 cup*
Tamarind	*big lemon-sized amount*
Sambar powder	*4 tsp*
Turmeric powder	*1 tsp*
Coriander leaves	*to decorate*
Salt	*to taste*
Oil	*as required*

To season

Mustard, fenugreek seeds, red chilli, asafoetida

Method

Pressure cook toor dhal and keep aside. Clean all the vegetables and cut into small pieces. In a big vessel cook the vegetables, with required salt and turmeric powder. Extract tamarind in 2 cups of water. When the vegetables are done, add the tamarind extract and sambar powder and boil well. Add the cooked toor dhal and bring to a boil again. Season with the given seasonings. Decorate with coriander leaves. This is prepared on the day of the festival Thiruvathirai as a side dish.

Ennai Kathirikai

(BRINJAL GRAVY IN OIL)

Ingredients

Purple brinjals	*500 gms, small, round ones*
Turmeric powder	*½ tsp*
Tamarind	*small lemon-sized amount*
Salt	*to taste*
Gingelly oil	*as required*
Coriander seeds	*2 tsp*
Channa dhal	*2 tbsp*
Urad dhal	*1 tbsp*
Dried red chillies	*3-4*
Fenugreek	*½ tsp*
Asafoetida	*a pinch*
Copra	*2 tbsp, grated, optional*
Salt	*to taste*

To season

Mustard seeds	*2 tsp*
Urad dhal	*1 tsp*
Curry leaves	*a few*

Method

Extract the tamarind juice after soaking it in 2 cups of water. Wash and slit brinjals into fours up to the end of the stalk without breaking the stem. Immerse in cold water. Shallow fry the ingredients for grinding and grind to a coarse powder. Stuff brinjals with powdered masala carefully. If any masala is left over, keep aside. Heat oil, add seasonings and arrange brinjals carefully. Lower heat and stir fry, turning over every now and then. Sprinkle leftover masala powder and turmeric powder. Cover and cook on low heat, sprinkling water if required. When brinjals are half done, add tamarind extract, salt (if necessary) and stir for some time. Add some more oil if required. Serve hot with rice.

Gudi Venkayilu (Andhra)

(STUFFED BRINJAL GRAVY)

Ingredients

Sambar onion	*250 gms, peeled and cut*
Tender brinjal	*500 gms, split lengthwise till halfway*
Tamarind extract	*1 tbsp*
Ginger-garlic paste	*1 tbsp*
Turmeric powder	*1 tsp*
Coriander powder	*2 tsp*
Chilli powder	*2 tsp*
Garam masala powder	*1 tsp*
Jeera	*1 tsp*
Mustard seeds	*1 tsp*
Curry leaves	*a few*

For masala

Fry in oil and grind to a paste:

Peanuts	*3 tbsp*
Urad dhal	*2 tsp*
Sesame seeds	*2 tsp*
Copra	*3 tbsp, grated*

Method

Stuff each brinjal with a little masala paste and keep aside. Heat oil in a kadai and add the jeera, mustard seeds and curry leaves. Add the remaining masala paste and ginger-garlic paste and fry. Add all the powders and then the stuffed brinjals and fry. Add the tamarind extract and required salt. Simmer for a few minutes till the gravy is blended well. This goes well with rice and aappam.

Kathirikkai Kadalai Paruppu Kuzhambu (Andhra)

(BRINJAL IN CHANNA DHAL GRAVY)

Ingredients

Tender brinjals	*500gms, cut into 4 pieces*
Channa dhal	*¾ cups*

Kathirikkai Kadalai Paruppu Kuzhambu (Andhra)

Cardamom	*1" piece*
Cloves	*2*
Curry leaves	*a few*
Onions	*2, sliced*
Ginger-garlic paste	*1 tsp*
Turmeric powder	*1 tsp*
Chilli powder	*1 tsp*
Coriander powder	*2 tsp*
Tamarind	*small lemon-sized amount*
Salt	*to taste*
Oil	*as required*

To grind

Grated coconut	*½ cup*
Poppy seeds	*2 tsp*
Tomatoes	*2*
Coriander leaves	*¼ cup*

Method

Pressure cook channa dhal till it is soft and cooked, but still retains its shape. Keep aside. In a heavy-bottom kadai heat a little oil. Shallow fry the cardamom, cloves and curry leaves. Sauté the onion slices. Add brinjals and sauté till the colour changes. Add the ginger-garlic paste and then turmeric, chilli, coriander powders and required salt sauté for 2 minutes. Add cooked dhal and tamarind extract. Let the gravy simmer till the brinjals are cooked. Add coconut paste boil for 5 more minutes. Serve with dosai, idli or rice.

Gudi Venkayilu (Andhra)

Mulangi Kondakadalai Paruppu Kuzhambu

(RADISH AND CHICKPEAS GRAVY)

Method

This is prepared with chickpeas and radish instead of channa dhal and brinjals in the same method used for kathrikkai kadalai paruppu kuzhambu.

Pooshnikkai Tengai Paal Koottu

(TENDER PUMPKIN IN COCONUT MILK)

Ingredients

Tender pumpkin	*500 gms*
Thick coconut milk	*½ cup*
Sugar	*2 tsp*
Rice flour	*1 tsp*
Salt	*to taste*
Oil	*as required*
To season	
Mustard seeds	*1 tsp*
Urad dhal	*1 tsp*
Green chillies	*2*

Method

Peel the pumpkin. Cut into thin, long pieces and cook with required salt. Add sugar while cooking. Mix rice flour with coconut milk and add to the vegetables. Boil for 2 minutes and season.

Note

Milk can be used instead of coconut milk, or a combination can be used.

Vazhakkai Koottu (Kerala)

(RAW BANANA COCONUT GRAVY)

Ingredients

Raw bananas	*3*
Moong dhal	*1 cup*
Grated coconut	*1 cup*
Red chillies	*2*
Chilli powder	*1 tsp*
Rice	*½ tsp*
Mustard seeds	*1 tsp*
Salt	*to taste*
Coconut oil	*as required*

Method

Peel the raw bananas and cut into small pieces. Keep in water. Dry roast moong dhal till you get a roasted flavour. Cook with required water, add the chopped bananas, chilli powder, red chillies and salt. Cook till done. Grind ¾ cup of coconut and rice to a smooth paste. Add this to the dhal banana mixture. Mix well and boil. Add the remaining grated coconut. Put off the flame. Garnish with mustard seeds fried in a little coconut oil.

Variation

Raw jackfruit can be used instead of banana.

Murungaikai Poricha Koottu

(DRUMSTICK DHAL GRAVY WITH COCONUT)

Ingredients

Moong dhal	*½ cup*
Drumstick	*4*
Turmeric powder	*a little*
Urad dhal	*1 tsp*
Jeera	*½ tsp*
Green chillies	*3*

Grated coconut	*½ cup*
Rice	*1 tsp*
Salt	*to taste*
Oil	*as required*
To season	
Mustard seeds, urad dhal, curry leaves	

Method

Cook moong dhal separately. Keep aside. Cut drumsticks into 4 pieces each and cook with required salt and turmeric powder in required water. Fry urad dhal to golden colour. Grind together fried urad dhal, jeera, green chillies, coconut and rice to a smooth paste. To the cooked drumstick, add the ground paste, cooked moong dhal, and required water. Boil together for a few minutes and season.

Note

Any vegetable like greens stalks, snake gourd, cluster beans can also be used.

Poricha Kuzhambu and Murugaikai Poricha Kootu are interchangeable names according to the region.

Beans Paal Kuzhambu (Andhra)

(BEANS GRAVY WITH MILK)

Ingredients

Cluster beans or any beans variety	*250 gms*
Cloves	*2*
Cinnamon	*2, 1" pieces*
Onion	*1, sliced*
Green chillies	*6*
Rava	*2 tbsp*
Ginger-garlic paste	*1 tsp*
Milk	*2 cups*
Salt	*to taste*
Oil	*as required*
Chopped coriander leaves	*to decorate*

Method

Cook the beans with required salt in minimum water. Heat oil in a kadai and shallow fry the cloves and cinnamon. Add onion and green chillies and fry. Then add rava and fry for a minute. Add ginger-garlic paste and fry for a minute. Add cooked beans and milk and simmer on low flame, till the gravy thickens. Decorate with chopped coriander leaves.

Mola Koottal (Kerala)

(VEGETABLE IN COCONUT GRAVY)

Ingredients

Pumpkin, drumstick, elephant yam	*250 gms*
Toor dhal	*½ cup*
Coconut	*½ cup, grated*
Jeera	*2 tsp*
Urad dhal	*2 tsp*
Chilli powder	*1 tsp*
Turmeric powder	*1 tsp*
Salt	*to taste*
Coconut oil	*as required*
To season	
Mustard seeds	*1 tsp*
Jeera	*1 tsp*
Urad dhal	*1 tsp*
Curry leaves	*a few*

Method

Pressure cook toor dhal. Keep aside. Roast urad dhal and jeera, grind with coconut to a smooth paste. Keep aside. Wash all vegetables, peel, cut into small pieces. Boil the vegetables with a pinch of turmeric powder, required salt and chilli powder. Add together cooked vegetables, cooked dhal and ground paste and if required a little water. Boil together for 5 minutes and season.

Note

Any other vegetable like snake gourd, chow-chow, greens and ash gourd can also be used.

Poricha Kuzhambu

Poricha Kuzhambu

(VEGETABLE GRAVY WITH COCONUT)

Ingredients

Any one of the vegetables like snake gourd, chow-chow, drumstick, cluster beans, broad beans, brinjals, amaranth stems	*500 gms, cut into pieces*
Toor dhal or moong dhal	*½ cup*
Sambar powder	*2 tsp*
Grated coconut	*½ cup, grind to a paste*
Rice flour	*½ tsp*
Salt	*to taste*
Oil	*as required*
To season	
Mustard seeds	*1 tsp*
Asafoetida	*a pinch*
Urad dhal	*1 tsp*
Curry leaves	*a few*

Method

Pressure cook dhal. Keep aside. Cook the vegetable with required salt and sambar powder. Add cooked dhal and ground coconut paste and boil together for a few minutes. If required add rice flour paste to make the gravy thick and then season.

Kaikurma (Andhra)

(VEGETABLE IN CURRY SAUCE)

Ingredients

Potatoes	*3, cut into cubes*
Carrots	*100 gms, cut into cubes*
Knookkal (knol-knol)	*100 gms, cut into cubes*
Beans	*100 gms, cut into long pieces*
Any other desired vegetables.	
Whole cinnamon	*2*
Cloves	*2*
Cardamom	*2*
Curry leaves and mint leaves	*a few*
Onions	*2, cut into slices*
Green chillies	*2, slit*
Turmeric powder	*1 tsp*
Lemon juice	*1 tsp*
Salt	*to taste*
Oil	*as required*

Masala I

Fry in a little ghee and grind together to a fine paste

Cloves	*1*
Cinnamon	*1*
Anise	*½ tsp*
Coriander seeds	*1 tbsp*
Onions	*3*
Green chillies	*10*
Ginger	*1 piece*
Garlic	*2*
Lastly mix coriander leaves	*¼ cup*

Masala II

Grind to a smooth paste

Coconut	*½ cup*
Poppy seeds	*2 tsp*
Tomatoes	*2*

Method

Heat oil in a cooker. Add the whole spices, curry leaves, mint leaves, onions, green chillies in this order. Add Masala I, turmeric powder and fry on very low heat, till the oil oozes out. Add the vegetables and fry for 2 minutes. Add and mix Masala II and required salt with the required quantity of water for the vegetables. Pressure cook till the vegetables are done. Mix the lemon juice. Serve hot with rice.

Kaikurma

(VEGETABLES IN CURRY SAUCE)

Ingredients

Carrot	*½ cup, cut into cubes*
Potato	*½ cup, cut into cubes*
Beans	*½ cup, cut into long pieces*
Cabbage	*½ cup, finely chopped*
Cauliflower	*½ cup, finely chopped*
Fresh peas	*½ cup*
Cinnamon	*2*
Cloves	*2*
Cardamom	*2*
Green chillies	*2, slit*
Onion	*½ cup, finely chopped*
Tomato	*½ cup, chopped*
Turmeric powder	*½ tsp*
Chilli powder	*1½ tsp*
Coriander powder	*2 tsp*
Thick curd	*1 cup*
Thick coconut milk	*½ cup*
Coriander leaves	*a few*
Salt	*to taste*
Oil	*as required*

Method

Boil vegetables till half done, keep aside. In a heavy-bottomed vessel, heat oil, sauté cinnamon, cloves, cardamom and then green chillies. Add onions and sauté, then add tomatoes. Add turmeric, chilli, coriander powders, sauté for a minute. Add curd and required salt. Now add boiled vegetables. Mix well and cook together for some time. Lastly, add the coconut milk. Put off the flame. Decorate with coriander leaves. Serve with rice or idiappam.

Uralaikizhangu Stew (Kerala)

(POTATO/VEGETABLE STEW)

Ingredients

Coconut	*1 cup, grated*
Potato	*250 gms*
Onions	*2, chopped*
Green chillies	*6*
Ginger-garlic paste	*2 tsp*
Salt	*to taste*
Oil	*as required*
To season	
Curry leaves	*a few*
Coconut oil	*a little*

Method

Extract milk from the coconut thrice, with the first extraction being the thickest and keep separately. Peel and cut the potatoes into cubes, cook in the thinnest coconut milk and keep aside. In a kadai, sauté onion to golden brown. Add ginger-garlic paste and sauté together. Add cooked potatoes, required salt and the thicker second-extraction of coconut milk. Boil together for a few minutes. Add the thickest first-extraction of coconut milk and when it comes to a boil put off the flame. Garnish curry leaves in a little coconut oil. This goes well with idiappam, aappam and rice.

Variation

Instead of potatoes, a combination of vegetables like beans, carrot, capsicum, peas can be used.

Kaikurma

Vazhapoo Vellam Koottu

(PLANTAIN FLOWER GRAVY WITH JAGGERY)

Ingredients

Plantain flower	*1*
Tamarind	*small lemon-sized amount*
Sambar powder	*1 tsp*
Turmeric powder	*½ tsp*
Grated coconut	*½ cup*
Jaggery	*large lemon-sized amount*
Rice flour	*1 tsp*
Salt	*to taste*
Oil	*as required*
To season	
Mustard seeds	*½ tsp*
Urad dhal	*1 tsp*
Channa dhal	*1 tsp*
Asafoetida	*a pinch*
Curry leaves	*a few*

Method

From the plantain flower, remove all the layers of red petals covering the finger-like flowers. Remove also the central stem from each finger-like flower. Finely chop all the flowers and keep soaked in thin tamarind extract or buttermilk. Drain completely and wash. Cook with required salt, turmeric powder and sambar powder till done. Pour in thick tamarind extract and jaggery. Allow jaggery to dissolve and mix well. Boil till it thickens. If required, add rice flour paste to thicken the gravy. Add grated coconut. Season with given seasonings.

Note

Vegetables like cluster beans, broad beans, brinjal, raw banana can also be used.

Vepampoo Rasam

(DRY NEEM FLOWER RASAM)

Ingredients

Dry neem flower	*½ cup*
Coriander seeds	*1 tbsp*
Toor dhal	*1 tbsp*
Red chillies	*10*
Tamarind	*small lemon-sized amount*
Asafoetida	*a pinch*
Mustard seeds	*1 tsp*
Salt	*to taste*
Ghee	*as required*

Method

Heat ghee in a kadai, shallow fry asafoetida, mustard seeds, toor dhal, coriander seeds and 2 red chillies. Extract tamarind in 3 cups of water. Pour tamarind extract and required salt into the kadai. Boil well till the raw flavour is removed. Heat ghee in a separate kadai and fry neem flowers till golden brown. Add this to the tamarind extract. Boil together for a few minutes. This is usually prepared for Tamil New Year's day.

Paruppu Rasam

(DHAL RASAM)

Ingredients

Tamarind	*small lemon-sized amount*
Rasam powder	*2 tsp*
Cooked toor dhal	*½ cup*
Salt	*to taste*
Ghee	*as required*
To season	
Mustard seeds	*½ tsp*
Pepper	*½ tsp, crushed*
Asafoetida	*a pinch*
Curry leaves	*a few*

Method

Extract tamarind in 3 cups of water. Boil together with rasam powder and required salt till the raw flavour is removed. Dissolve the cooked dhal in half cup water and add. Bring to one boil. Season with the above seasonings.

Thakkali Rasam

(TOMATO RASAM)

Method

This is prepared in the same way as paruppu rasam, except that tomatoes are added before adding dhal.

Elumicha Rasam

(LEMON RASAM)

Ingredients

Toor dhal	*½ cup*
Lemon	*2*
Green chillies	*6*
Rasam powder	*1 tsp*
Asafoetida	*a pinch*
Mustard seeds	*½ tsp*
Red chillies	*2*
Curry leaves	*a few*
Salt	*to taste*
Ghee	*as required*
Coriander leaves	*to decorate (chopped)*

Method

Pressure cook dhal. Add 3 cups of water and boil together with rasam powder, green chillies, asafoetida and required salt. Season with mustard seeds, red chillies and curry leaves. Remove from fire. Squeeze the lemon into it. Mix well. Decorate with coriander leaves.

Seeraga Rasam

(JEERA RASAM)

Ingredients

Tamarind	*small lemon-sized amount*
Rasam powder	*1 tsp*
Salt	*to taste*
Ghee	*as required*

Soak for 10 minutes and grind to a paste

Coriander seeds	*2 tsp*
Toor dhal	*1 tsp*
Jeera	*1 tsp*
Pepper	*1 tsp*
Red chillies	*2*
Curry leaves	*a few*

To season

Mustard seeds, curry leaves

Method

Extract tamarind in 3 cups of water. Add required salt and rasam powder, boil till the raw flavour is removed. Add the ground paste and bring to one boil. Put off the flame and season.

Kottu Rasam

(INSTANT RASAM)

Ingredients

Tamarind	*small lemon-sized amount*
Asafoetida	*a pinch*
Mustard seeds	*½ tsp*
Toor dhal	*1 tsp*
Red chillies	*3*
Curry leaves	*a few*
Salt	*to taste*
Ghee	*as required*

Method

Extract tamarind in 3 cups of water. In a heavy-bottomed vessel, lightly fry mustard seeds, red chillies, toor dhal and curry leaves in a little ghee. Pour the tamarind extract, required salt and asafoetida. Boil together for a few minutes.

Optional

Tomatoes can also be used.

Poondu Rasam

Poondu Rasam

(GARLIC RASAM)

Ingredients

Tamarind	*small lemon-sized amount*
Mustard Seeds	*½ tsp*
Curry Leaves	*a few*
Salt	*to taste*
Ghee	*as required*

Shallow fry in a little ghee and grind to a coarse paste

Coriander seeds	*2 tsp*
Channa dhal	*1 tsp*
Red chillies	*2*
Pepper	*½ tsp*
Jeera	*½ tsp*
Garlic	*4 cloves*

Method

Extract tamarind in 3 cups of water. Boil with required salt, till the raw flavour is removed. Add the ground paste. Bring to one boil. Remove from fire and season with mustard seeds and curry leaves fried in a little ghee.

Optional

Chopped tomatoes can be added if desired.

Milagu Rasam

(PEPPER RASAM)

Ingredients

Tamarind	*small lemon-sized amount*
Salt	*to taste*
Ghee	*as required*

Shallow fry in a little ghee and grind to a powder

Pepper	*1 tsp*
Jeera	*½ tsp*
Toor dhal	*1 tsp*
Red chilli	*1*

To season

Mustard seeds, curry leaves, red chilli

Method

Extract tamarind in 3 cups of water. Boil with required salt till the raw flavour is removed. In a kadai, sauté the ground powder in a little ghee. Add to the tamarind extract. When it is boiling, season with given ingredients and turn off the flame.

Mysore Rasam (Karnataka)

Ingredients

Tamarind	*small lemon-sized amount*
Toor dhal	*¼ tsp*
Salt	*to taste*
Ghee	*as required*

Shallow fry in a little ghee and grind to a paste

Coriander seeds	*2 tsp*
Jeera	*1 tsp*
Fenugreek seeds	*½ tsp*
Pepper	*½ tsp*
Channa dhal	*½ tsp*
Grated coconut	*¼ cup*

To season

Mustard seeds, curry leaves

Method

Pressure cook toor dhal and keep aside. Extract tamarind in 3 cups of water. Add required salt and boil till the raw flavour is removed. Add the ground paste and cooked dhal. Boil together for a few minutes. Season with given seasonings.

DRY DISHES

Along with gravy dishes, fresh vegetable dishes cooked without any gravy form an important part of a south Indian meal. These dishes are called poriyal in Tamil Nadu and palya in Andhra and Karnataka. Dry dishes are generally of two types. The first are prepared with root vegetables like potato, yam etc, cooked with spices and using oil to make them crispy. Green vegetables like cabbage, beans and so on are chopped and boiled with the required salt and then seasoned. This type of dish is fairly mild and bland.

Only a few dry dishes are included in this section as samples. Any other vegetable can be prepared as a dry item, according to one's taste.

Sembu Ilai Curry

(COLOCASIA LEAVES CURRY)

Ingredients

Broad colocasia leaves	*10, approximately*
Toor dhal	*2 tbsp*
Channa dhal	*2 tbsp*
Whole urad dhal	*2 tbsp*
Moong dhal	*2 tbsp*
Red chillies	*8*
Asafoetida	*a pinch*
Turmeric powder	*a pinch*
Mustard seeds	*½ tsp*
Urad dhal	*1 tsp*
Salt	*to taste*
Oil	*as required*

Method

Wash and soak all the dhals together for 1 hour. Drain and grind all the dhals together with red chillies, asafoetida, turmeric powder and required salt into a smooth firm paste (sprinkle water if needed). Keep aside. Cut and remove stalk from the leaves. Wash each leaf and wipe dry. Spread the paste evenly on the back of the leaf. Roll each leaf tightly. Arrange the rolls on greased idli plates and steam cook till done. To test, the leaf changes its colour and a needle comes clean through the paste without sticking. After cooling, cut each roll into 2” slices. Keep aside. Heat oil in a kadai. Lightly fry mustard seeds and urad dhal. Add the prepared slices and sauté carefully, till the slices become crisp.

Urulai Kizanigu Roast

(POTATO ROAST)

Ingredients

Potatoes	*500 gms*
Mustard seeds	*½ tsp*
Asafoetida	*a pinch*
Turmeric powder	*1 tsp*
Chilli powder	*2½ tsp*
Salt	*to taste*
Oil	*as required*

Method

Boil potatoes till tender in a little water or pressure cook. After cooling, peel and dice into cubes. Heat 2-3 tsp of oil in a kadai. Fry mustard seeds till they splutter and add potato cubes. Add asafoetida, turmeric powder, chilli powder and required salt. Mix well with a flat ladle without breaking the potatoes. Keep simmering till the potatoes become crisp.

Note

Vegetables like yam, elephant yam, colocasia and raw banana can also be prepared as a roast.

Vazakkai Podi

(MASHED RAW BANANA)

Ingredients

Raw banana	*2*
Red chillies	*6*
Toor dhal	*2 tsp*
Urad dhal	*2 tsp*
Salt	*to taste*
Oil	*as required*
To season	
Mustard seeds	*1 tsp*
Asafoetida	*a pinch*

Method

Cook raw banana whole or in halves in water or pressure cook till done. Peel the skin carefully, press and break the cooked banana into coarse pieces. Keep aside. Fry red chillies, toor dhal and urad dhal in a little oil and grind to a coarse powder. Mix this powder and required salt with the cooked banana and season.

Vazakkai Podi

Vazappoo Paruppu Usili

(DRY PLANTAIN FLOWER DHAL CURRY)

Ingredients

Plantain flower	*1*
Toor dhal	*1 cup*
Channa dhal	*1 cup*
Red chillies	*3*
Green chillies	*3*
Asafoetida	*a pinch*
Salt	*to taste*
Oil	*as required*

To season

Mustard seeds, turmeric powder, curry leaves

Method

Peel off the layers of red petals covering the finger-like flowers of the plantain flower. Remove also the central stem from each finger-like flower. Then chop finely all the flowers and keep soaked in thin tamarind extract or buttermilk. Cook the chopped flowers in water with required salt. Drain completely and keep aside. Wash and soak the dhals for 2 hours and drain. Grind dhals together with chillies, asafoetida and required salt, coarsely (water may be sprinkled if needed). Steam cook the same in greased idli plates. After cooling, break the dhal into tiny pieces. In a kadai, lightly fry the given seasonings in oil. Add broken dhal and shallow fry, stirring constantly on a low flame. Add the cooked plantain flower to the dhal. Mix and fry together on a low flame for a few more minutes. Turn off the flame.

Note

In paruppu usili, instead of plantain flowers, cluster beans, onions, beans and cabbage can be used.

Masala Chepankizangu

(MASALA COLACASIA ROAST)

Ingredients

Small colocasia (arbi)	*500 gms*
White sesame seeds	*1 tsp*
Chilli powder	*1 tsp*
Turmeric powder	*½ tsp*
Garam masala	*1 tsp*
Salt	*to taste*
Oil	*as required*
Chopped coriander leaves	*to decorate*

Method

Cook colocasia till it is three-fourths tender. Cool and peel the skin, cut into equal sized slices. Heat oil in a kadai and deep fry the colocasia slices till golden brown. Keep aside. In a kadai, fry some sesame seeds till they splutter, then add chilli powder, turmeric powder and garam masala. Add the fried slices and required salt. Mix and sauté for a few minutes. Sprinkle chopped coriander leaves before serving.

Urulai Kizanigu Podimaas

(POTATO SCRAMBLED)

Ingredients

Potatoes	*500 gms*
Mustard seeds	*1 tsp*
Urad dhal	*1 tsp*
Channa dhal	*1 tsp*
Green chillies	*4, cut*
Curry leaves	*a few*
Lemon	*1, optional*
Salt	*to taste*
Oil	*as required*
Chopped coriander leaves	*to decorate*

Method

Clean the potatoes and cook till tender. Peel and mash the potatoes into soft pieces using your hands. Heat a little oil in a kadai. Fry mustard seeds, urad dhal, channa dhal, green chillies and curry leaves. Add mashed potatoes and required salt and mix well. Before serving sprinkle chopped coriander leaves on the potato. Finally lemon juice may be mixed into the dish.

Note
This is a non-spicy and relatively oil-free dish made with potato or banana, to accompany spicy gravies.

Muttai Kose Curry

(CABBAGE CURRY)

Ingredients

Cabbage	*500 gms*
Mustard seeds	*½ tsp*
Urad dhal	*1 tsp*
Red or green chilli	*1 or 2*
Salt	*to taste*
Oil	*as required*
Grated coconut	*1 tbsp, optional*

Method

Wash and cut cabbage into thin strips, or grate. Heat 1 tsp oil in a kadai. Let mustard seeds splutter, add urad dhal and chilli. Add cabbage, sprinkle water and cook till half done. Mix in required salt and cook till tender. Sauté for a few minutes. Mix the coconut and serve.

Note
All fresh vegetables or even greens can be prepared this way, for example, broad beans, knol-knol, cluster beans, cauliflower, carrot, etc.

MIXED RICE DISHES

In south India, rice is the staple food. Apart from plain boiled rice, which generally accompanies gravies to enhance taste, various other types of rice like the lemon flavoured chitrannam or the popular bisibele bath are also prepared.

Bisibele Bath (Karnataka)

Bisibele Bath (Karnataka)

(MIXED VEGETABLE RICE)

Ingredients

Rice	*1 cup*
Toor dhal	*½ cup*
Potato	*2, cut into pieces*
Carrot	*2, cut into pieces*
Beans	*a few, cut into pieces*
Brinjals	*2, cut into pieces*
Peas	*1 tbsp*
Small onions	*10, peeled*
Tamarind	*medium lemon-sized amount*
Turmeric powder	*a pinch*
Asafoetida	*a pinch*
Salt	*to taste*
Ghee or oil	*as required*

For masala

Shallow fry in a little oil and grind to a powder

Coriander seeds	*3 tbsp*
Channa dhal	*2 tbsp*
Urad dhal	*½ tbsp*
Red chillies	*10*
Pepper	*½ tsp*
Fenugreek seeds	*½ tsp*
Cardamom	*2*
Cinnamon	*1*
Cloves	*2*
Grated coconut	*3 tbsp*
Poppy seeds	*3 tsp, optional*

To season

Mustard seeds, curry leaves

To decorate, cashew nuts

Method

Cook all the vegetables with a little salt. Keep aside. Pressure cook dhal and rice together with 3 cups of water adding turmeric powder and required salt. Keep aside. Extract tamarind juice after soaking tamarind in 1 cup of water. Heat oil, fry the onions till golden brown. Add thick tamarind extract, required salt, asafoetida and boil. Now add cooked vegetables and powdered masala, boil together for a few minutes. Blend in the cooked rice carefully in this boiling extract and simmer for a few minutes. Serve hot with any raita and pappad.

Thengai Sadam

(COCONUT RICE)

Method

Prepare like coconut sevai, using cooked rice instead of sevai.

Elumicha Sadam

(LEMON RICE)

Method

Prepare like lemon sevai, using cooked rice instead of sevai.

Puliam Sadam

(TAMARIND RICE)

Ingredients

Cooked rice	*as required, each grain is separate*
To prepare pulikaichal (tamarind sauce)	
Tamarind	*big lemon-sized amount*
Red chillies	*6*
Channa dhal	*1 tsp*
Mustard seeds	*1 tsp*
Asafoetida	*a pinch*
Turmeric powder	*a pinch*
Curry leaves	*a few*
Salt	*to taste*
Gingelly oil	*2 tbsp*
Fenugreek seeds	*½ tsp, dry roast and powder*
Sesame seeds	*1 tsp, dry roast and powder*

Method

Extract thick tamarind juice with 2 cups of water. In a heavy-bottomed vessel, heat the oil till mustard seeds splutter. Shallow fry channa dhal, red chillies, asafoetida, turmeric powder and curry leaves. Add tamarind extract and required salt. Boil for 15 minutes, till it thickens. Mix the prepared powder. Turn off the flame. This can be stored for about a week to 10 days. Tamarind rice is prepared by mixing cooked rice with this sauce as and when required.

Vankai Annamu (Andhra)/Vangi Bath (Karnataka)

(BRINJAL RICE)

Ingredients

Rice	*1 cup*
Mustard seeds	*1 tsp*
Whole red chillies	*2*
Asafoetida	*a pinch*
Curry leaves	*a few*
Green brinjal	*3, cut into pieces lengthwise*
Thick tamarind extract	*2 tbsp*
Turmeric powder	*a pinch*
Powdered jaggery	*1 tsp*
Lemon juice	*1 tsp*
Ghee	*1 tsp*
Salt	*to taste*
Gingelly oil	*as required*
For masala powder	
Dry roast and grind coarsely	
Cinnamon	*1" piece*
Cardamom	*2*
Cloves	*2*
Coriander seeds	*2 tbsp*
Channa dhal	*1 tbsp*
Urad dhal	*1 tbsp*
Red chillies	*7*
Fenugreek seeds	*½ tsp*
Jeera	*½ tsp*
Copra	*½ cup, to be added last*

Fried cashew nuts and chopped coriander leaves to decorate.

Method

Pressure cook the rice with 2½ cups of water. Each grain should be separate. Heat oil and ghee in a kadai, add mustard seeds and let them splutter. Shallow fry red chillies, asafoetida and curry leaves. Add the brinjal. Fry till almost done. Add tamarind extract, prepared masala powder, turmeric powder, required salt and jaggery. Cook for 4 to 5 minutes. Pour this mixture on cooked rice, mix well. If required, add some more masala powder and sauté together for a few minutes. Mix lemon juice and decorate. Serve with raita and pappad.

Kadamba Sadam (Karnataka)

(MIXED RICE WITH VEGETABLES)

Ingredients

Basmati rice	*1½ cups*
Kabuli channa	*1 tbsp*
Whole moong dhal	*1 tbsp*
Black-eyed beans	*1 tbsp*
Broad beans	*50 gms*
Elephant yam	*50 gms, peeled and cut into pieces*
Sweet potato	*3, peeled and cut into pieces*
Pumpkin	*50 gms, cut*
Tamarind	*small lemon-sized amount*
Turmeric powder	*1 tsp*
Salt	*to taste*

For masala

Shallow fry in a little oil and grind to a powder

Coriander seeds	*3 tbsp*
Channa dhal	*1½ tbsp*
Whole urad dhal	*1 tbsp*
Red chillies	*6*
Asafoetida	*1 tsp*

To season

Ghee	*4 tbsp*
Mustard seeds	*1 tsp*
Jeera	*1 tsp*
Red chilli	*1, slit*
Curry leaves	*a few*
Chopped coriander leaves	*to decorate*

Method

Soak kabuli channa, moong dhal and black-eyed beans for a minimum of 8 hours. Drain and pressure cook with required salt and keep aside. Cook rice in 3 cups of water. Keep aside. Prepare tamarind extract in 2 cups of water. In a heavy-bottomed vessel, heat ghee. Season with given seasonings. Pour tamarind extract. Add all the vegetables, a pinch of turmeric powder and required salt. Boil till vegetables are done. Add masala powder and cooked dhals. Boil for a few more minutes till gravy thickens. Mix the cooked rice and simmer for a few minutes together. Decorate and serve hot with pappad and raita.

Note

Any combinations of vegetables like brinjals, ladies finger, drumstick, raw banana can also be used.

Small vadas can also be added: soak 2 tbsp urad dhal for 1 hour. Grind to a thick batter with required salt. Make small vadas and deep fry.

Kothamalli Sadam

(CORIANDER RICE)

Ingredients

Rice	*1 cup*
Jeera	*½ tsp*
Salt	*to taste*
Gingelly oil	*as required*

To grind

Grind together to a paste

Coriander leaves	*1 cup*
Mint leaves	*1 tbsp*
Ginger	*1″ piece*
Onion	*1*
Green chillies	*2*

Method

Soak rice for 10 minutes and pressure cook with 2½ cups of water. Each grain should be separate. Heat a kadai. Shallow fry jeera and ground paste for a few minutes. Mix in the cooked rice and required salt. Sauté for a few more minutes. Serve with pappad and raita.

Note

If desired 1 cardamom, 1 clove, 1 cinnamon and 2 bay leaves can also be shallow fried together with the jeera.

Pudina Sadam

Pudina Sadam

(MINT RICE)

Method

This is prepared in the same way as Kothamalli Sadam, except that the quantity of mint is increased to 1 cup and that of coriander leaves is reduced to 1 tbsp.

Mangai Sadam I

(MANGO RICE)

Ingredients

Rice	*1 cup*
Raw mango	*1 large-sized*
Carrot	*1 small-sized*
Fenugreek seeds	*½ tsp*
Salt	*to taste*
Gingelly oil	*as required*
To season	
Mustard seeds	*1 tsp*
Curry leaves	*a few*
Red chillies	*3*
Green chillies	*5*
Turmeric powder	*a pinch*

Method

Cook the rice with 2½ cups of water. Each grain should be separate. Keep aside. Peel the raw mango and carrot. Finely grate them separately. Heat a little oil in a kadai. Shallow fry all the seasoning ingredients. Add grated mango and carrot. Sauté and cook till done with required salt and water. Put off the flame. Mix the cooked rice with this, using a fork. Roast the fenugreek seeds, powder finely and sprinkle on the mango rice.

Mangai Sadam II

(MANGO RICE)

Method

Cook the rice with 2½ cups of water. Each grain should be separate. Keep aside. Grind together a small piece of ginger, 2 cloves of garlic, half cup grated coconut, 6 red chillies, a piece of cinnamon, 2 cloves and one cardamom. Lightly fry mustard seeds, urad dhal and curry leaves. Add the ground paste and shallow fry. Add the grated mango and carrot and sauté together. Continue as in mangai sadam I.

Kootan Choru

(MIXED VEGETABLE RICE)

Ingredients

Rice	*1 cup*
Toor dhal	*½ cup*
Brinjal	*1, diced into cubes*
Raw banana	*1, diced into cubes*
Potatoes	*1, diced into cubes*
Drumstick	*1, cut into 3" pieces*
Turmeric powder	*a pinch*
Asafoetida	*a pinch*
Chilli powder	*2 tsp*
Onion	*1, sliced thinly*
Tomato	*1, sliced thinly*
Salt	*to taste*
To season	
Mustard seeds	*1 tsp*
Urad dhal	*1 tsp*
Curry leaves	*a few*
Ghee	*1 tsp*
Drumstick leaves	*a few, optional*
Oil	*as required*

Method

Cook all vegetables with a little turmeric powder, asafoetida, chilli powder and required salt. Keep aside. Add tomato and onion slices to the dhal and pressure cook together. Strain both the dhal and the vegetables after cooking, to remove the stock. Measure this stock and add water to make a total of 2½ cups. Add this water to rice and pressure cook. Mix the cooked dhal and vegetables in the rice well, keep simmering for a few minutes. Fry given seasonings in ghee. Mix well and serve.

Bahala Bath

(CURD RICE)

Ingredients

Rice	*1 cup*
Curd	*1 cup*
Milk	*1 cup*
White butter	*1 tbsp*
Salt	*to taste*
To season	
Mustard seeds	*½ tsp*
Asafoetida	*a pinch*
Green chillies	*3, slit*
Ginger	*1" piece, cut*
Curry leaves	*a few*
Oil	*as required*

Method

Pressure cook rice with 3 cups of water to a very soft consistency. Mash the hot rice with a little salt using a wooden ladle. Add butter, curd and milk. Mix and blend together and season with given seasonings.

Semiya Bahala Bath

(VERMICELLI CURD DISH)

Method

Prepare as in curd rice, using 100 gms of vermicelli instead of rice.

Bahala Bath

SAVOURY SHORT EATS

There are many crispy short eats unique to south India, like murukku and cheedai. Very simple ingredients like rice flour and dhal flour are used to prepare these. Even though they are deep fried, they are all-time favourites.

Preparation of processed rice flour used in many short eats and sweets

Wash and soak rice for 15 minutes. Drain completely and dry on a white cloth for 30 minutes in the shade. Pound in a flour mill into a smooth flour. Dry the flour on the cloth for 15 minutes in the shade. Sieve through a fine sieve and store in an airtight container until needed.

Preparation of roasted urad dhal powder used in many short eats and sweets

Dry roast 1 cup urad dhal on a hot pan to a light pink colour. Pound in the mixie to a smooth flour. Sieve and store in an airtight container.

Note

These flours can be used for up to 10-15 days.

If the flour is too old, the preparation will take on a dark colour.

Mullu Thenkuzhal

Mullu Thenkuzhal

(MULLA MURUKKU)

Ingredients

Processed rice flour	*2 cups*
Moong dhal	*½ cup*
Channa dhal	*½ cup*
Butter	*1 tsp*
Salt	*to taste*
Oil	*for deep frying*

Method

Dry roast moong dhal and channa dhal separately to a pinkish colour. Grind to a smooth powder separately. In a large bowl mix together 2 cups of processed rice flour, ½ cup of channa dhal flour and ½ cup of moong dhal flour. Add butter and required salt. Sprinkle water a little at a time as required and prepare a stiff dough. Using the given mould plate, prepare mullu thenkuzhal.

Kara Boondhi

(SPICY CHANNA DHAL FLOUR BEADS)

Ingredients

Channa dhal flour	*1½ cups*
Rice flour	*1 cup*
Chilli powder	*2 tsp*
Baking soda	*a pinch*
Asafoetida	*a pinch*
Salt	*to taste*
Oil	*for deep frying*
To decorate	
Broken cashew nuts	*20*
Curry leaves	*a few*

Method

In a large bowl, mix together all ingredients and add enough water to make a thick batter. Heat oil in a kadai. Hold the kara boondhi ladle (perforated and with a long handle) closely over the hot oil. Pour a tbsp of batter on the disc and, using a flat spoon, rub the batter through the holes in the disc very quickly. The batter will fall in the form of tiny beads into the hot oil. Cook the beads to a golden colour, turning them often with a perforated ladle. Remove from oil, straining out the oil completely. Repeat the process with the rest of the batter. Fry cashew nuts and curry leaves and mix in the kara boondhi. This process is to be done very carefully.

Varukadalai

(FRIED CHANNA DHAL)

Ingredients

Whole channa	*1 cup*
Red chilli powder	*1 tsp*
Asafoetida	*a pinch*
Salt	*to taste*
Oil	*for deep frying*
Fried cashew nut	*1 tbsp, optional*

Method

Soak the channa overnight. When it is soft, spread the dhal on a white cloth and dry in shade. Heat oil in a kadai to a moderate temperature. Deep fry the channa in it a handful at a time. Transfer to a bowl, straining out the oil completely. Mix chilli powder, asafoetida, and required salt with the fried dhal, while it is still warm.

Vennai Cheedai

(BUTTER CRISPY RICE BALLS)

Method

Add more butter (3-4 tsp) to the flour in the above dough and roll similarly. The size of the cheedais should be very small.

Note

Whenever any cheedai is prepared, one should be very careful. Cheedais, being ball-shaped, will burst open in the hot oil if there are any dust, sand or stone particles in the flour. So rice used for these should be cleaned meticulously.

Kara Sev

(SPICY AND CRISPY NOODLE-LIKE SNACK)

Ingredients

Channa dhal flour	*1 cup*
Rice flour	*½ cup*
Red chilli powder	*1 tsp*
Pepper powder	*½ tsp*
Asafoetida	*½ tsp*
Butter	*1 tsp*
Salt	*to taste*
Oil	*for deep frying*

Method

Mix all the given ingredients in a bowl. Sprinkle water little by little as required and prepare a stiff dough. Divide the dough into cylindrical balls. In the meanwhile, heat oil in a kadai. Keep each ball in the murukku-maker with the specified mould plate. Press this in moderately hot oil in a circular motion. Deep fry till golden brown.

Nippattu (Andhra)

Method

Nippattu are prepared in the same manner. They are thicker than Thattai (Pg 97) and curry leaves should be added to the dough.

Uppu Cheedai

(SALTED CRISPY RICE BALLS)

Ingredients

Processed rice flour	*1 cup*
Roasted urad dhal flour	*1½ tsp*
Channa dhal	*1 tsp*
Asafoetida	*a pinch*
Coconut pieces	*1 tsp, optional*
Butter	*1 tsp*
Salt	*to taste*
Oil	*as required*

Method

Soak channa dhal for 10 minutes and drain. Dissolve the required salt and asafoetida in water. Keep aside. Dry roast the rice flour on a hot pan for 2-3 minutes. To test whether the flour is roasted properly: Hold a pinch of flour between the thumb and forefinger. Draw a line with it on the floor. The line should fall smoothly without any breaks. Sieve rice flour, mix it well in a bowl with the urad dhal flour. Mix in butter, channa dhal and coconut pieces. Sprinkle the salt water gradually and prepare a firm dough. Divide the dough and roll into little marble sized balls. Spread them on a white cloth for about 15-30 minutes. Heat oil in a kadai. Deep fry the cheedais to a golden brown colour.

Varutha Mochai

(FRIED FIELD BEANS)

Ingredients

Field bean seeds	*1 cup*
Chopped cashew nuts	*1 tbsp*
Red chilli powder	*½ tsp*
Salt	*to taste*
Oil	*for deep frying*

Method

Soak dry field bean seeds overnight. If they are fresh seeds, soak in warm water for 2 hours only. Peel the outer skin of soaked beans and dry up the moisture by spreading the seeds over a cloth in shade. Deep fry (a handful at a time) in hot oil till crisp and golden. Strain oil completely. Fry cashew nuts and add to it. Sprinkle the required salt and chilli powder over the fried beans while they are still warm so that the powders stick to it easily and mix well.

Kara Sev

Ribbon Pakoda

(RIBBON SHAPED SNACK)

Ingredients

Channa dhal flour	*2 cups*
Rice flour	*1 cup*
Red chilli powder	*2 tsp*
Asafoetida	*a pinch*
Butter	*1 tbsp*
Salt	*to taste*
Oil	*for deep frying*

Method

Mix all the ingredients. Add water gradually as required and prepare a stiff dough. Divide into cylindrical balls. Meanwhile, heat oil in a kadai. Stuff the balls one by one in the murukku maker with specified mould plate (see utensils) and press the mould in the hot oil in a circular motion, carefully. Deep fry till ribbon pakodas are crisp.

Omappodi

(THIN CRISPY SEV)

Ingredients

Channa dhal flour	*1 cup*
Rice flour	*1/3 cup*
Tymol seeds	*½ tsp, crushed*
Salt	*to taste*
Oil	*for deep frying*

Method

Mix all the ingredients in a bowl. Sprinkle required water and prepare a stiff dough. Divide into cylindrical balls. Meanwhile, heat oil in a kadai to a moderate temperature. Stuff the balls one by one in the murukku-maker with the specified mould plate and press it in the hot oil in a circular motion, with care. Deep fry till it is cooked crisp.

Note

Kara Omappodi is prepared by mixing chilli powder with other ingredients to prepare the dough.

Poondu Karasev

(GARLIC KARASEV)

Ingredients

Channa dhal flour	*1 cup*
Rice flour	*½ cup*
Garlic	*6 flakes*
Green chillies	*4*
Butter	*1 tsp*
Salt	*to taste*
Oil	*as required*

Method

Grind garlic and green chillies into a paste. Dissolve the paste in water and filter. Keep aside. Mix all other ingredients together in a bowl. Add the filtered chilli water a little at a time as required and prepare a stiff dough. Using the specified mould plate, prepare poondu karasev.

Thenkuzhal

(CRISPY NOODLE-LIKE SNACK)

Ingredients

Processed rice flour	*1 cup*
Roasted urad dhal flour	*1 tsp*
Jeera	*½ tsp*
Asafoetida	*½ tsp*
Butter or ghee	*1 tsp*
Salt	*to taste*
Oil	*for deep frying*

Method

Mix all the given ingredients. Sprinkle water a little at a time as required and prepare a stiff dough. Using the specified mould plate, prepare thenkuzhal.

Thattai

(CRISPY RICE DISCS)

Ingredients

Processed rice flour	*1 cup*
Roasted urad dhal flour	*1½ tsp*
Channa dhal	*1 tsp*
Chilli powder	*1 tsp*
Asafoetida	*a pinch*
Vanaspathi or butter	*1 tsp*
Baking soda	*a pinch*
Salt	*to taste*
Oil	*for deep frying*

Method

Soak channa dhal for 10 minutes and drain. Sieve rice flour and mix it with urad dhal powder in a bowl. Blend in the butter and add required salt, chilli powder, asafoetida and channa dhal. Add water gradually and prepare a stiff smooth dough. Divide and roll into small balls. Spread a white cloth and flatten each ball into a circular shape on it, by patting slowly with your fingers. Make the discs as thin as possible and prick with a needle or fork to make tiny holes on them. Heat oil in a kadai and deep fry a few at a time, till golden brown.

Note

Crushed peanuts or cashew nuts may be used instead of soaked channa dhal. Instead of chilli powder, pepper powder or green chilli paste can be used.

Kai Murukku

(CRISP RICE SPIRALS)

Ingredients

Processed rice flour	*1 cup*
Roasted urad dhal flour	*1 tsp*
Jeera	*½ tsp*
Asafoetida	*a pinch*
Butter	*1 tbsp*
Salt	*to taste*
Oil	*for deep frying*

Method

Dry roast rice flour till hot. Do not let the colour change. Sift through a fine sieve. Mix rice flour, urad dhal flour, asafoetida, jeera with required salt and butter. Prepare a firm dough, sprinkling required water. Spread a white cloth on the floor. Take a little dough in oiled fingers and spin out into small spirals, twisting the dough continuously, on the cloth. Make 2-3 whirls in each murukku. Each murukku will resemble a spiral, made of rows of twisted chord. Repeat the process with the rest of the dough and allow to dry for some time. Meanwhile heat oil in a kadai. Transfer each murukku onto a greased plate and gently slide into hot oil. Deep fry to a golden brown. Murukku is an auspicious snack for weddings in all southern states.

Note

Since the above method of making murukku by hand can be cumbersome, these days a murukku press is used, though the result is not as good.

Mullu Murukku

(STAR-SHAPED CRISPY SNACK)

Ingredients

Processed rice flour	*1 cup*
Moong dhal	*1 cup*
Channa dhal	*1 cup*
Butter	*1 tsp*
Salt	*to taste*
Oil	*for deep frying*

Method

Dry roast moong dhal and channa separately to a golden pink colour. Grind each dhal to a smooth powder. In a large bowl mix together 1 cup of processed rice flour, 1 cup of channa dhal flour and 1 cup of moong dhal flour (i.e. equal amounts of all flours). Add butter and required salt. Sprinkle water a little at a time and make a stiff dough. Using the specified mould plate, prepare mullu murukku.

ACCOMPANIMENTS

South Indian cuisine is well renowned for the variety of accompaniments it includes. Pickles are hot, spicy accompaniments which go well with plain rice, curd rice and tiffin dishes. Commonly used vegetables in the pickles are raw mango, types of lemon and gooseberry, ginger etc., although, any other suitable vegetable can be used. Pickles can usually be stored up to a year if properly prepared and handled. Traditionally, pickles are a must in south Indian meals. Pickles are recommended to be eaten only in small quantities due to the large amounts of oil, spice and salt they contain.

Dry powders, or podi, are ready mixes which serve as instant food. Particularly in Andhra Pradesh, various types of podi prepared from different ingredients are always kept handy to serve a ready mal. A little ghee or gingelly oil is always used with it.

Chutneys are pastes which accompany all tiffin and tiffin snacks as a side dish.

Thogaiyals (Tamil Nadu) or pachadis (Andhra) are thick chutneys which are used to accompany rice dishes. They are very healthy as they have high fibre and low calorie content, and use very little oil. The vegetables in the thogaiyal are not cooked for very long.

Vadu Mangai

(TENDER MANGOES)

Ingredients

Tender mango with stems	*1 kg*
Red chillies	*100 gms*
Mustard seeds	*50 gms*
Asafoetida	*1 tsp*
Rock salt	*300 gms*

Method

Wash the tender mangoes well and wipe with a cloth. Sprinkle a layer of rock salt at the bottom of a jar. Then fill a layer of tender mangoes. Repeat the process, until all the mangoes are layered like this. The top layer should be salt. Close the mouth of the jar tightly. Set aside for 3 days, shaking the jar now and then. Meanwhile, sun dry or dry roast mustard seeds, red chillies and asafoetida and grind to a coarse powder. Add and mix this powder to the salted mangoes and mix thoroughly, using a wooden ladle. The speciality of this pickle is that there is no oil at all. The pickle will be ready to eat after 10 days.

Avakkai Mangai (Andhra)

(VERY SPICY MANGO PICKLE)

Ingredients

Sour raw mangoes (special mangoes with hard shell seeds)	*1 kg*
Chilli powder	*1 cup*
Mustard seeds powdered	*1 cup, dry roasted and*
Fenugreek seeds powdered	*1 tbsp, dry roasted and*
Salt	*as required*
Gingelly oil or mustard seed oil	*as required*

Avakkai Mangai (Andhra)

Method

Wash the mangoes and wipe dry with a cloth. Cut open and remove the seeds. Then cut into 8 or 12 pieces each (it is important to retain the hard shell while cutting). Coat the pieces with a little oil. Combine chilli powder, mustard seed powder and fenugreek powder with salt and mix some of it into the oiled pieces evenly. In a clean jar, spread one layer of prepared mangoes. Then sprinkle 1 tsp of the spice powder and pour a little oil over this. Repeat this process till all the mango pieces are layered like this. Cover tightly and set aside for 3 days. Stir well. Pour over 2-3 tbsp of oil, so that the oil covers the pickle completely. Keep covered tightly. Stir well now and then. The pickle is ready for use after 2 weeks.

Thidir Mangai Urugai
(INSTANT MANGO PICKLE)

Ingredients

Raw sour mangoes	*2, cut into small cubes*
Chilli powder	*2 tsp*
Asafoetida	*1 tsp*
Salt	*as required*
Gingelly oil	*as required*
Mustard seeds	*to season*

Method
Add salt and chilli powder to the cubed mangoes and toss well. Heat 2 tsp of oil. Allow mustard seeds and asafoetida to splutter. Pour over the mangoes and blend well. This pickle is instantly ready but can be stored only for 3 or 4 days.

Note
Gooseberry and lime pickle may also be prepared in the same way.

Mangai Thokku
(GRATED MANGO PICKLE)

Ingredients

Raw mangoes	*2*
Chilli powder	*3 tsp*
Turmeric powder	*1 tsp*
Fenugreek powder	*1 tsp, roasted*
Mustard seeds	*to season*
Asafoetida	*to season*
Gingelly oil	*2 tbsp*
Salt	*as required*

Method
Peel the mangoes, grate and marinate in salt. Set aside for 3 hours. Heat oil, allow mustard seeds to splutter and add asafoetida. Add grated mango and cook for some time on a slow fire. Mix in chilli powder, turmeric powder and fenugreek powder and stir well. Pour in 5 tsp of oil and cook till the oil separates from the rest of the mixture. This can be eaten immediately.

Note
Large gooseberries can also be prepared using the same method and recipe.

Mangai Inji Elumichai
(MANGO GINGER IN LIME)

Ingredients

Tender mango ginger	*125 gms, peeled and cut into slices*
Tender green chillies	*25 gms, finely chopped*
Turmeric powder	*a pinch*
Lime juice	*1 tbsp*
Salt	*1 tsp*
Oil	*as required*

Method
Combine all the above ingredients and toss well. Pickle is ready for use after a day and can be stored for up to 10 days.

Note
Normal ginger can also be prepared in the same way.

Pickles

Kathirikkai Kothsu

(THIN BRINJAL GRAVY)

Ingredients

Green brinjal	*3, cut into pieces*
Onion	*2, cut into pieces lengthwise*
Thick tamarind extract	*1 cup*
Moong dhal	*½ cup*
Mustard seeds	*½ tsp*
Green chillies	*2*
Asafoetida	*a pinch*
Curry leaves	*a few*
Jaggery	*a little, optional*
Salt	*to taste*
Oil	*as required*

Fry in a little oil and grind to a coarse powder

Coriander seeds	*2 tsp*
Fenugreek seeds	*½ tsp*
Channa dhal	*1 tsp*
Red chillies	*4*

Method

Pressure cook moong dhal. Keep aside. Heat oil, shallow fry mustard seeds, green chillies, curry leaves, asafoetida. Add onion and sauté to a golden colour. Add brinjal and sauté for a minute. Pour in the tamarind extract and add required salt. Boil till vegetables are done (water can be added if required). Add the ground powder and cooked dhal. Mix well. Boil for a few minutes. Add jaggery.

Note

This can be prepared without onion too.

This goes well with pongal, rice uppuma and idli.

Thakkali-vengaya Chutney

(ONION-TOMATO CHUTNEY)

Ingredients

Onions	*2, cut*
Tomatoes	*2, cut*
Red chillies	*2*
Tamarind	*a little*
Urad dhal	*½ tsp*
Salt	*to taste*
Oil	*as required*

Method

Shallow fry onion and tomato. Keep aside. Fry red chillies and urad dhal in a little oil separately. Grind all ingredients together to a coarse paste. This goes well for idli, dosa and ada.

Note

This can also be prepared with only tomato or only onion.

Verusennaga Chutney (Andhra)

(PEANUT CHUTNEY)

Ingredients

Roasted peanuts	*1 cup, peeled*
Red chillies	*6*
Fried gram	*1 tbsp*
Tamarind	*a little*
Jaggery	*a little*
Salt	*to taste*
Oil	*as required*
To season	
Mustard seeds	*½ tsp*
Urad dhal	*½ tsp*
Red chilli	*1*
Curry leaves	*a few*

Method

Fry red chillies in a little oil. Grind all the ingredients to a coarse paste with a little water and season.

Thengai Chutney

Thengai Chutney

(COCONUT CHUTNEY)

Ingredients

Grated coconut	*½ cup*
Green chillies	*3*
Fried gram	*½ cup*
Salt	*to taste*
Oil	*as required*

To season

Mustard seeds, curry leaves, urad dhal, asafoetida

Method

Grind all the ingredients together with a little water and season. This goes well with all the tiffin varieties.

Note

A small piece of ginger and/or 1-2 garlic flakes can also be ground together.

Gongura Chutney (Andhra)

(SORREL LEAVES CHUTNEY)

Ingredients

Gongura leaves	*1 cup*
Red chillies	*5*
Green chillies	*5*
Fenugreek seeds	*½ tsp*
Asafoetida	*a pinch*
Urad dhal	*1 tsp*
Mustard seeds	*½ tsp*
Jaggery	*a little optional*
Salt	*to taste*
Oil	*as required*

Method

Wash and drain the gongura leaves. Dry roast in a hot kadai for a few minutes. Keep aside. Heat a little oil in a pan and fry the chillies, fenugreek seeds and urad dhal. Grind all the ingredients together to a coarse paste with a little water. Let mustard seeds splutter in a little oil. Add the ground paste and fry for 2 minutes. This chutney can be used for up to 3 to 4 weeks. This goes well with idli, dosa, pesarettu, rice.

Allamu Chutney (Andhra)

(GINGER CHUTNEY)

Ingredients

Ginger	*50 gms*
Tamarind	*a little*
Red chillies	*15*
Whole urad dhal	*1 tbsp*
Coconut/copra	*1 tbsp, optional*
Salt	*to taste*
Oil	*as required*

Method

Heat a little oil in a pan, fry the ginger, red chillies and urad dhal, each separately. Grind all the ingredients together to a coarse paste with water. This chutney is mainly served with pesarettu.

Cigappu Chutney

(RED CHILLIES CHUTNEY)

Ingredients

Coconut	*½ cup*
Channa dhal	*2 tbsp*
Red chillies	*4*
Salt	*to taste*
Oil	*as required*
Mustard seeds	*to season*

Method

Heat a little oil in a pan, fry red chillies and channa dhal. Grind all the ingredients to a coarse thick paste, sprinkling water, and season. This goes well with all tiffin dishes.

Thengai Thuvaiyal

(COCONUT PASTE)

Thuvaiyal is a thick chutney, which is mixed with plain rice. To prepare this no water/or very little water should be used.

Ingredients

Grated coconut	*1 cup*
Tamarind	*small lemon-sized amount*
Red chillies	*6*
Urad dhal	*3 tsp*
Asafoetida	*a pinch*
Salt	*to taste*
Oil	*as required*

Method

Fry red chillies and urad dhal in a little oil. Grind together all the ingredients to a coarse paste, sprinkling water if required.

Pudina Thuvaiyal

(MINT PASTE)

Method

Wash and clean the leaves and tender stalks of mint. Prepare like coconut paste.

Kothamalli Thuvaiyal

(CORIANDER LEAVES PASTE)

Method

Wash and clean the leaves and tender stalks of coriander. Prepare like coconut paste.

Karugeppilai Thuvaiyal

(CURRY LEAVES PASTE)

Method

Wash and clean the leaves and tender stalks of curry leaves. Prepare like coconut paste.

Pudina Chutney

(MINT CHUTNEY)

Ingredients

Mint leaves	*1 cup*
Fried gram	*1 tbsp*
Green chillies	*5*
Tamarind	*a little*
Mustard seeds	*½ tsp*
Urad dhal	*½ tsp*
Salt	*to taste*
Oil	*as required*

Method

Wash and drain the mint leaves, dry roast in a hot kadai for a few minutes. Grind with the rest of the ingredients to a coarse paste, sprinkling water as needed. Season with mustard seeds and urad dhal.

Thengai Thuvaiyal

Kothamalli Chutney

(CORIANDER LEAVES CHUTNEY)

Method

In this recipe, instead of mint leaves, coriander leaves can be used or a combination of mint and coriander leaves.

Pachai Milagai Chutney

(GREEN CHILLIES CHUTNEY)

Ingredients

Green chillies	*100 gms*
Tamarind	*a little*
Fenugreek seeds	*½ tsp*
Urad dhal	*1 tsp*
Jaggery	*a little*
Mustard seeds	*½ tsp*
Asafoetida	*a pinch*
Salt	*to taste*
Gingelly oil	*as required*

Pachai Milagai Chutney

Method

Heat a little oil, shallow fry urad dhal, fenugreek seeds and green chillies. Grind together all the ingredients with a little water, to a coarse paste. Heat oil in a kadai. Let mustard seeds splutter, then add the ground paste and fry for 2 minutes. This can be stored for 3-4 days. This goes well with all tiffin dishes and plain rice.

Puli Milagai

(TAMARIND CHILLI PICKLE)

Ingredients

Tender green chillies	*100 gms*
Tamarind	*big lemon-sized amount*
Fenugreek seeds	*1 tsp*
Mustard seeds	*½ tsp*
Asafoetida	*a pinch*
Turmeric powder	*a pinch*
Jaggery powder	*1 tsp*
Salt	*to taste*
Oil	*as required*

Method

Slit green chillies lengthwise partially. Extract thick tamarind juice. Dry roast fenugreek seeds and powder. Heat oil in a kadai, allow mustard seeds to splutter. Add asafoetida, turmeric powder and slit green chillies and fry for a minute. Add tamarind juice and required salt. Boil for a few minutes. Add fenugreek powder and jaggery. Boil together till the mixture becomes semi-solid. This goes well with all the tiffin dishes like idli, dosai etc.

Puli Inji

(TAMARIND GINGER PICKLE)

Method

This is prepared like tamarind chilli pickle using a combination of 100 gms ginger and 100 gms green chillies, instead of green chillies only.

Paruppu Thuvaiyal

(DHAL PASTE)

Ingredients

Toor dhal	*½ cup*
Red chillies	*2*
Tamarind	*a little, optional*
Salt	*to taste*
Oil	*as required*

Method

Fry toor dhal in a little oil to a golden brown colour and fry red chillies with it. Grind together all the ingredients to a coarse paste, sprinkling a little water.

Note

A combination of equal portions of toor dhal and channa dhal can also be used in this recipe.

Kathirikkai Thuvaiyal

(BRINJAL PASTE)

Ingredients

Brinjal	*1 large sized*
Red chillies	*8*
Whole urad dhal	*3 tsp*
Tamarind	*small lemon-sized amount*
Asafoetida	*a pinch*
Mustard seeds	*½ tsp*
Salt	*to taste*
Oil	*as required*

Method

Apply a little oil on the brinjal and roast directly over a reduced flame carefully. All the sides should be roasted evenly. After cooling, peel the skin carefully, wetting your fingers now and then. Keep aside. Fry red chillies and urad dhal in a little oil. Grind together all the ingredients. Mash the brinjal with your fingers and mix with the ground ingredients.

Note

In the same method, chow-chow, green tomato, cabbage, ridge gourd, snake gourd elephant yam can also be used. Cut the vegetables, with the skin, into big pieces and shallow fry in a little oil for 2-3 minutes and continue as in previous recipe.

Idli Milagai Podi

Idli Milagai Podi

(CHILLI POWDER FOR IDLI)

Ingredients

Sesame seeds	*100 gms*
Urad dhal	*250 gms*
Channa dhal	*150 gms*
Red chillies	*50 or 75 gms*
Asafoetida	*a little*
Salt	*to taste*
Oil	*1 tsp*

Method

Dry roast sesame seeds, then fry other ingredients (except salt) in a little oil and grind to a coarse powder. Mix required salt. This can be stored in an airtight container up to a month.

Note

A teaspoon of sugar or jaggery powder may also be mixed into it.

Paruppu Podi

Vepampoo Podi

(NEEM FLOWER POWDER)

Ingredients

Neem flower	*1 cup*
Urad dhal	*1 tsp*
Coriander seeds	*1 tsp*
Red chillies	*6*
Asafoetida	*little*
Ghee	*1 tsp*
Salt	*to taste*

Method

Heat ghee in a kadai. Turn off the flame and fry neem flowers in the heated ghee carefully. Keep aside. Shallow fry all ingredients in a little oil and grind to a coarse powder.

Paruppu Podi

(TOOR DHAL POWDER)

Ingredients

Toor dhal	*1 cup*
Red chillies	*4*
Curry leaves	*a few*
Asafoetida	*a little*
Salt	*to taste*
Oil	*1 tsp*

Method

Shallow fry all ingredients in a little oil and grind to a coarse powder.

Karugepillai Podi

(CURRY LEAVES POWDER)

Ingredients

Curry leaves	*2 cups*
Urad dhal	*4 tsp*
Channa dhal	*1 tsp*
Coriander seeds	*½ tsp*
Red chillies	*6*
Tamarind	*a little*
Jaggery	*a little*
Salt	*to taste*

Method

Wash and dry curry leaves. Shallow fry all ingredients in a little oil and grind to a coarse powder.

Manathakkali Podi

(BITTER BERRY PODI)

Ingredients

Dry black night shade	*1 cup*
Urad dhal	*6 tsp*
Red chillies	*5*
Pepper	*1 tsp*
Jeera	*1 tsp*
Asafoetida	*½ tsp*
Salt	*to taste*
Oil	*½ tsp*

Method

Dry roast pepper and jeera. Keep aside. In a little oil shallow fry all other ingredients and grind to a coarse powder.

Khus-khus Podi

(POPPY SEEDS POWDER)

Ingredients

Poppy seeds	*100 gms*
Urad dhal	*2 tsp*
Channa dhal	*2 tsp*
Red chillies	*12*
Asafoetida	*little*
Salt	*to taste*
Oil	*as required*

Method

Shallow fry all ingredients in a little oil and grind to a coarse powder.

Kothamalli Vodhi Podi

(CORIANDER SEEDS POWDER)

Ingredients

Coriander seeds	*1 cup*
Urad dhal	*½ tsp*
Channa dhal	*½ tsp*
Red chillies	*4*
Asafoetida	*a little*
Tamarind	*small lemon-sized amount*
Salt	*to taste*
Oil	*1 tsp*

Method

Shallow fry all ingredients in a little oil and grind to a coarse powder.

Kothamalli Vodhi Podi

SWEETS

In south India, sweets form a very important part of a meal, be it an everyday lunch, or a more formal dinner or an occasion like a wedding. Sweets indicate celebration, and particular sweets are also used as offerings, Naivedyam, after the performance of poojas.

In today's health conscious world, people are increasingly careful about the quantity of fat and sugar that they consume. Our lifestyle does not allow us to consume sweets as liberally as before. However, it is a commonly held misconception that sweets become tastier by adding more sugar and ghee. The actual taste of the sweet dish lies in how and when the ghee and sugar are added, and the correct cooking time.

The sweets are prepared with sugar or jaggery which are either mixed into the dish or prepared as a syrup and used. The taste of each sweet differs only because of the different consistency of the syrup used.

Sugar and jaggery always contain dirt and sand particles. So before using, ensure they are cleaned as below:

In a heavy-bottomed kadai, mix the sugar or jaggery in a little water. The ratio of sugar or jaggery to water may be 4:1. Heat just enough to dissolve it, stirring now and then. Filter and remove all insoluble dirt and then use. Another method is to boil and add a few drops of milk. Before reaching the correct consistency, all insoluble dirt will froth and float on top. Remove this with a spoon.

The following are the different consistencies of the syrup. Always dip fingers in cold water before testing the hot syrup.

Thin Syrup - Sugar dissolves completely and syrup suddenly clears and gets a shine.

Sticky Syrup - When dipped in the syrup, your finger will feel sticky.

One-String Consistency - Dip forefingers and thumb in the syrup. When fingers are removed from the syrup, one thin string is formed between them up to 2 inches long (used for badhusha, kunjaladu, etc.)

Two-String Consistency - When tested as above, 2 strings are formed.

Three-String Consistency - When tested as above, 3 or more thicker strings are formed (used for puttu, etc.)

Gathering Consistency - Pour 1 tsp of syrup in cold water. It settles down at the bottom and can be gathered with fingers (for some types of halwa, burfi, etc.)

Soft Ball Consistency - Drop 1 tsp of syrup in cold water and roll between the fingers. The syrup forms a soft ball (for adhirasam, etc)

Hard Ball Consistency - When tested like above, the syrup forms a hard ball (for peanut balls, etc.)

Appi Payasam (Karnataka)

(POORI KHEER)

Ingredients

Maida	*2 tbsp*
Milk	*4 cups*
Sugar	*1 cup*
Oil	*for deep frying*
To flavour	
Cardamom powder	*½ tsp*
Saffron	*a pinch*

Method

Knead the maida with required water to a stiff smooth dough. Divide and roll out into very thin small pooris. Heat oil in a kadai and deep fry the pooris till crispy. Remove, draining completely. In a separate kadai, boil milk and add sugar, cardamom powder and saffron into it. Immediately after frying, dip hot pooris in hot water for 15 seconds. Remove and crush and add to the boiling milk. Boil together for a few minutes more and turn off the flame.

Javvarisi Payasam

(SAGO KHEER)

Ingredients

Sago	*½ cup*
Sugar	*¼ cup*
Jaggery	*¼ cup*
Thick coconut milk	*1 cup*
Diluted coconut milk	*2 cups*
Boiled milk	*½ cup*
To flavour	
Fried cashew nuts	*a few*
Saffron	*a pinch*
Edible yellow colour	*a few drops, optional*

Method

Wash and soak sago in 1 cup of diluted coconut milk for 3-4 hours till the grains swell. Cook in diluted coconut milk till three-fourths done (water can be added if required). In a heavy-bottomed vessel, dissolve the jaggery and sugar in a cup of water. Add the sago in it and boil till sago is cooked fully and becomes transparent and soft to touch. Add milk and all flavouring agents and boil for a few minutes more. Now add thick coconut milk. Bring to one boil and turn off the flame.

Kadalai Paruppu Payasam

(CHANNA DHAL KHEER)

Ingredients

Channa dhal	*½ cup*
Grated coconut	*1 tbsp*
Cashew nuts	*5, optional*
Jaggery or sugar	*1 cup*
Milk	*1 cup*
To flavour	
Cardamom powder	*1 tsp*
Fried cashew nuts	*1 tsp*

Method

Dry roast channa dhal in a hot pan and pressure cook till done. When the dhal has cooled down, grind with grated coconut and cashew nuts into a paste, adding water if required. In a heavy-bottomed vessel, boil the jaggery in 1 cup water. Add ground channa dhal paste and boil till the paste is blended well. Add the milk, bring to one boil and add cardamom powder and roasted cashew nuts. Cool and serve.

Paal Payasam

(MILK KHEER)

Ingredients

Milk	*1 litre*
Sugar	*½ cup*
Rice	*1 tbsp*
To flavour	
Fried cardamom powder	*1 tsp*
Cashew nuts and raisins	*a few*

Method

Dry roast rice in a hot kadai and pressure cook in 2 cups of milk and water. In a separate kadai, boil the rest of the milk till it is reduced to three-fourths of its volume. Mash and add the cooked rice in this and boil together for a few more minutes, stirring frequently, till it is blended well. Add sugar and boil till it dissolves completely. Add cardamom powder, fried cashew nuts, raisins. Cool and serve.

Paruppu Thootham (Andhra)

(MOONG DHAL KHEER)

Ingredients

Moong dhal	*1 cup*
Powdered jaggery	*2 cups*
Cardamom powder	*1 tsp*
Roasted coconut pieces	*to decorate*

Method

Dry roast moong dhal in a hot pan and pressure cook. Boil jaggery in 2 cups of water till it becomes a little thick. Mash and add the cooked dhal with cardamom powder and boil for a few minutes. Decorate and serve after cooling. This is a traditional diet for elders fasting on vratha days and for those on a very simple diet.

Kozhakattai

(STEAMED AND STUFFED RICE BALLS)

For filling

Powdered jaggery	*¾ cup*
Grated coconut	*1 cup*
Cardamom powder	*1 tsp*

Heat oil in a kadai, add jaggery, coconut, and cardamom. Sauté and cook, stirring constantly for some time on a high flame till the mixture becomes stiff. Let it cool.

For kozhakattai

Processed rice flour	*1 cup*
Salt	*a pinch*
Gingelly oil	*1 tsp*

Heat 1½ cups of water in a heavy-bottomed kadai. Add salt and oil. When it starts to boil, reduce flame. Add the flour slowly, stirring constantly with a ladle, so that lumps do not form. Cook for about 5 minutes. Turn off the flame. Keep covered with a wet cloth for some time. When cool, knead well to a smooth dough (sprinkle water if required) using oiled fingers. Divide into small balls. Using the thumb and forefinger, shape the balls gradually into a cup shape. Keep a little filling in the middle and carefully close it from all sides. Shape into a bud shape and seal well. Arrange on a greased idli plate and steam cook for 10 minutes. Transfer to a shallow plate immediately. Allow to cool without disturbing and serve.

Note

This is a very auspicious sweet and is prepared for Ganesh Chaturthi and other poojas, as an offering.

Paal Payasam

Semiya Payasam

Semiya Payasam

(VERMICELLI KHEER)

Ingredients

Vermicelli	*½ cup*
Sugar	*¾ cup*
Milk	*1 litre*
Ghee	*1½ tsp*
To flavour	
Fried cashew nuts, raisins	*1 tsp*
Cardamom powder	*½ tsp*
Saffron	*a pinch*

Method

Break and fry vermicelli in 1 tsp ghee for 2 minutes. Add boiling water and cook till done. Meanwhile boil milk till it is reduced to three-fourths. Add this thick milk to the cooked vermicelli and cook on a low flame for a few minutes. Gently mix in sugar and heat till it dissolves and put off the flame. Mix all the flavouring agents. This can be served hot or cold.

Rava Payasam

(RAVA KHEER)

Method

Prepared in the same manner as vermicelli kheer.

Aval Payasam

(RICE FLAKES KHEER)

Method

Prepared in the same manner as vermicelli kheer.

Thengai Paal Payasam

(COCONUT MILK KHEER)

Ingredients

Thick coconut milk	*1 cup*
Diluted coconut milk	*1 cup*
Channa dhal	*1 tbsp*
Moong dhal	*1 tbsp*
Rice	*1 tbsp*
Powdered jaggery	*2 cups*
Roasted coconut pieces	*to decorate*

Method

Dry roast channa dhal, moong dhal and rice in a hot pan and pressure cook together. Boil jaggery in 2 cups of water till it becomes a little thick. Mash and add the cooked dhals and diluted coconut milk. Boil together for a few minutes. Now add the thick coconut milk. Bring to one boil. Add roasted coconut pieces and serve after cooling.

Thengai Paal Payasam

Palada Pradaman (Kerala)

(STEAMED RICE KHEER)

Ingredients

Raw rice	*½ cup*
Maida	*1 tsp*
Coconut oil	*1 tsp*
Milk	*2 litre*
Sugar	*½ cup*
Small banana leaves	*as required*

Method

Wash and soak rice for 30 minutes. Grind to a smooth consistency like a dosa batter. Mix maida and coconut oil in the batter. On the reverse of small banana leaves, spread the batter with fingers into thin layers. Roll the banana leaves one by one separately and tie with small strings. Arrange the rolls carefully on idli plates and steam them. When the colour of the leaves changes to a light brown, turn off the flame. Transfer them into cold water immediately. As required, change the cold water twice or thrice. The leaves and rice layers will separate in the water itself. Throw away the leaves and the strings. Wash the rice flour layers in cold water, changing the water 3-4 times. Change the water till the layers become tough. Now cut the layers into small pieces. Keep aside. Meanwhile, boil the milk separately in a heavy-bottomed vessel and reduce it to three-fourths its volume. Add the cooked rice pieces to the boiling milk. Add sugar and let it boil for some more time, till the kheer is blended well. Serve after cooling.

Chakka Pradaman (Kerala)

(JACKFRUIT KHEER)

Ingredients

Jackfruit pieces	*15*
Jaggery	*500 gms*
Thick coconut milk	*1 cup*
Diluted coconut milk	*2 cups*
Roasted coconut pieces	*1 tbsp*
Cardamom powder	*1 tsp*
Ghee	*as required*

Method

Cook the jackfruit in sufficient water, until tender. Drain and then grind to a smooth paste. In a heavy-bottomed vessel, put 3 tsp ghee, jaggery and ground paste. Cook this, stirring constantly till the moisture is absorbed and it becomes thick. (This paste can be stored up to a week and can be used as and when required). Dissolve this paste in diluted coconut milk and boil for 10-15 minutes. Pour the thick coconut milk and bring to a boil again. Add in roasted coconut pieces and cardamom powder and serve.

Sajjapalu (Andhra)

(RAVA STUFFED POORI)

Ingredients

Fine rava	*½ cup*
Maida or wheat flour	*1 cup*
Sugar	*1 cup*
Ghee	*3 tbsp*
Cardamom powder	*2 tsp*
Oil	*for deep frying*

For dough

Knead maida into a stiff dough with enough water and 1 tbsp ghee. Keep aside.

For filling

Heat 1 tbsp ghee in a kadai and roast rava to a reddish brown colour. Pour 1 cup of water and cook rava, stirring constantly. When half done, add sugar and 1 tbsp of ghee and cardamom powder. Cook till totally done. Turn off the flame.

Continue as in previous recipe for thengai sojji aappam.

Paal Kozhakattai

(STEAMED RICE BALLS IN KHEER)

Ingredients

Raw rice	*1 cup*
Parboiled rice	*1 cup*
Grated coconut	*½ cup*
Powdered jaggery	*1 ½ cups*
Diluted coconut milk	*2 cups*
Thick coconut milk	*1 cup*
Cardamom	*3 tsp*
Ghee	*1 tsp*
Coconut oil	*2 tsp*

Method

Wash and soak both rice together for 3 hours. Drain, add coconut and grind to a thick batter. Heat kadai, add oil, pour the batter, stirring constantly so that lumps do not form. Cook for a few minutes, transfer to a tray when it becomes a thick dough. After cooling, add 1 tbsp jaggery and a pinch of cardamom powder. Mix well and divide into tiny balls. Steam cook in an idli cooker for 10 minutes. In a heavy-bottomed vessel, pour the diluted coconut milk and the rest of the jaggery. Boil for some time. Add the steamed rice balls. Boil for 3-5 minutes. Add the thick coconut milk, cardamom powder and ghee. Bring to one boil and when cold, serve.

Paalpaniyaram

(FRIED RICE BALLS IN KHEER)

Ingredients

Rice	*1 cup*
Urad dhal	*½ cup*
Thick coconut milk	*1 cup*
Sugar	*1 cup*
Cardamom powder	*1 tsp*
Milk	*½ cup*
Oil	*for frying*

Method

Wash and soak dhal and rice for 3 hours. Grind together to a smooth dough. Divide the dough into small balls. Heat oil and deep fry the balls till golden brown. Immediately after frying, dip hot balls in hot water for 15 seconds. Remove. In the meanwhile, boil milk, with sugar and cardamom powder, until sugar dissolves. Add thick coconut milk, then the fried balls and bring to a boil. Serve immediately (if kept for a long time balls become soggy).

Thirattupaal

(CONDENSED MILK GOVA)

Ingredients

Whole milk	*1 litre*
Sugar	*1 cup*
Cardamom powder	*1 tsp*
Ghee	*1 tsp*

Method

In a heavy-bottomed vessel, heat milk till it boils. On a low flame, simmer the milk for 15-20 minutes, stirring continuously till milk reduces to half its original quantity. Add sugar, cardamom powder and ghee and simmer for some more time, till the mixture condenses to a thick paste. This can be stored for up to a week.

Note

Unsweetened gova is prepared in the same way without adding sugar and cardamom powder and is used to prepare many kinds of sweets.

Holige Poli (Karnataka)

(SWEET ROTIS WITH DHAL FILLING)

For the dough

Maida	*2 cups*
Sugar	*2 tbsp*
Ghee	*2 tsp*
Oil	*as required*

Sieve maida, add powdered sugar. Make a hole in the middle. Pour ghee in it and mix well. Add 2 tsp of oil and sprinkle water a little at a time, as required. Knead into smooth pliable dough. Smear a little oil over the dough and keep aside for 6 hours, covering it with a wet cloth.

To prepare poli

Divide the dough into small balls. Roll into circular pooris. Keep 1 tbsp of filling in the centre of each poori. Close from all the edges, covering the filling totally to make a big ball again. Sprinkle a little maida and once again roll into a thin poori. Heat a dosa tawa. Roast each poli on it, pour a little ghee around it and cook till both sides are done. Before serving, sprinkle a little hot ghee.

For filling

Channa dhal	*1 cup*
Powdered sugar	*1 cup*
Cardamom powder	*a pinch*

Wash and soak channa dhal for 2 hours. Pressure cook for 15 minutes. Do not overcook. Drain water completely and grind dhal in the mixie till mashed. Add sugar and cardamom and grind once more till completely mixed. Keep aside.

Obbattu (Karnataka)

(SWEET ROTIS)

Method

This is done the same way as holige poli but instead of using sugar with channa dhal, jaggery (the same amount) is used with channa dhal to prepare obbattu.

Obbattu (Karnataka)

Paal Poli

(MILK POLI)

Ingredients

Fine rava	*1 cup*
Milk	*1 litre*
Sugar	*1 cup*
Powdered cashew nuts and almond	*1 tsp*
Ghee	*1 tbsp*
Oil	*for deep frying*
To flavour	
Cardamom powder	*½ tsp*
Saffron	*a pinch*

Method

Mix together rava and ghee, knead well to make a smooth dough. After 15 minutes knead the dough again to make it pliable and smooth and keep covered in a wet cloth for 2-3 hours. Divide and roll out thin pooris from the dough. Heat oil in a kadai and deep fry the pooris. Meanwhile, boil milk till it is reduced to three-fourths its volume. Add sugar, saffron, cardamom, nuts and boil for a few minutes more. Dip the hot pooris in the boiling milk and remove immediately with a ladle. Fold and arrange on a plate side by side. Decorate with a little saffron on top.

Suruttu Poli

(POLI ROLLS)

Ingredients

Fine rava or cheroti rava	*1 cup*
Sugar	*1 cup*
Cardamom	*5*
Cashew nuts and almond	*½ cup*
Whole cloves	*10 to 15*
Ghee	*1 tbsp*
Oil	*for deep frying*
Saffron	*to decorate*

Method

Mix together rava and ghee, knead well to make a smooth dough. After 15 minutes knead the dough again, keep covered in a wet cloth for 2-3 hours. Meanwhile, grind cashew nuts, almonds, cardamom and sugar together. Keep aside. Divide and roll out thin pooris. Heat oil in a kadai. Deep fry the pooris on a low flame. The pooris should not become crisp. Drain and transfer to a shallow plate. On each poori, spread 1 tsp of filling along one edge and roll it like a Swiss roll. Secure the rolls by inserting a clove through each. Arrange side by side on a serving tray and decorate with a little powdered sugar, saffron and almonds.

Thengai Poli

(COCONUT POLI)

For dough

Maida	*2 cups*
Powdered sugar	*2 tsp*
Turmeric powder	*a pinch*
Ghee	*2 tsp or as required*
Oil	*as required*

Sieve maida, add powdered sugar and turmeric powder. Make a hole in the middle. Pour ghee in it and mix well. Add oil and sprinkle water a little at a time as required. Knead into smooth pliable dough. Smear a little oil over the dough and keep aside for 6 hours, covering it with a wet cloth.

For filling

Grated coconut	*2 cups*
Powdered jaggery	*1 cup*
Raw rice	*1 tbsp*
Fried gram powder	*1 tsp (if required)*
Cardamom	*3*

Soak rice for 10 minutes. Grind coconut and cardamom along with jaggery and drained rice. In a hot kadai, sauté the coconut mixture till moisture is absorbed completely (if there is excess moisture, required fried gram powder can be added). Divide into small balls. Keep aside.

To prepare poli

Roll out circular pooris from the dough. Keep 1 tbsp of filling in the centre of each poori, close from all the edges, covering the filling totally to make a big ball again. Sprinkle a little maida and once again roll into a thin poori. Roast each poori on a hot tawa. Pour a little ghee around it and cook till both sides are done. Before serving, sprinkle a little hot ghee on the polis.

Ila Adai (Kerala)

(SWEET RICE DISH STEAMED IN PLANTAIN LEAVES)

Ingredients

Rice	*3 cups*
Grated coconut	*2 cups*
Jaggery	*300 gms*
Rice flakes	*2 tsp*
Cardamom powder	*1 tsp*
Plantain leaves	*4, cut into small size*

Method

Soak rice flakes for a few minutes and drain. Heat a heavy-bottomed kadai, sauté coconut, rice flakes and jaggery together. Cook till this becomes thick. Mix cardamom powder. Keep aside. Meanwhile wash and soak rice for 30 minutes and grind to a smooth thick batter. Pour this batter in thin layers on small plantain leaves, like dosas. Spread a little filling on the dosa. Fold the leaves into 4. Carefully arrange on a idli plate side by side. Steam cook in idli cooker till done. When done, the leaves change to a brown colour. Serve along with the folded leaf, steaming hot.

Suyyan

(COCONUT STUFFED BALLS)

For dough

Whole urad dhal	*½ cup*
Channa dhal	*1 tsp*
Rice	*1 tsp*
Salt	*a pinch, optional*
Oil	*for deep frying*

Soak urad dhal with channa dhal and rice for 1 hour. Drain and grind well to a smooth, soft batter, sprinkling water. Keep aside.

For filling

Powdered jaggery	*¾ cup*
Grated coconut 1	*cup*
Cardamom powder	*1 tsp*
Oil	*for deep frying*

Heat a kadai, add jaggery, coconut, and cardamom. Sauté and cook, stirring constantly for some time on a high flame till the mixture becomes stiff. Divide into small balls.

To prepare suyyan

Dip each coconut ball in urad dhal batter (as we do for bondas) and deep fry till golden brown on a slow fire.

Note

Instead of preparing a separate whole urad dhal dough for the covering, suyyans can be easily prepared, by dipping the balls in available dosa batter at home.

Thengai Sojji Aappam

(COCONUT STUFFED POORI)

Ingredients

Maida or wheat flour	*1 cup*
Ghee	*1 tbsp*
Grated coconut	*1 cup*
Sugar	*¾ cup*
Cardamom powder	*1 tsp*
Roasted cashew nuts	*a few*
Oil	*for deep frying*

For dough

Knead maida into a stiff dough with enough water and ghee. Keep aside.

For filling

Grind coconut to a smooth paste. Prepare a thick sugar syrup till two-string consistency. Add cardamom powder and coconut paste and cook well till moisture is absorbed completely.

To prepare aappams

Divide the dough into small balls. Flatten out each ball into a thin poori, on a greased plantain leaf, using fingers. Keep a tsp of filling in the middle and close it from all sides. Flatten this again into a small thick poori. Heat oil in a kadai. Deep fry the prepared stuffed pooris on a slow fire, till both sides become golden brown.

Rava Paal Kesari

(MILK KESARI)

Method

This is prepared as rava kesari, except that the rava is cooked in milk instead of water.

Gothumai Halwa

(WHEAT HALWA)

Ingredients

Samba wheat	*1 cup, approx. 150 gms*
Sugar	*2 cups*
Orange colour	*a few drops*
Ghee	*as required*
Rose essence	*a few drops*
Chopped nuts	*to decorate*

Method

Wash and soak the wheat for a minimum of 4 hours. Grind with 2-3 cups of water in the mixie. Strain and extract thick milk in 2 stages. Allow this milk to stand without disturbing, overnight (or for a minimum of 7-8 hours). By now, all the excess water will stand on the top. Drain out this excess water carefully. Measure the remaining thick paste. For 1 cup of paste, mix in 1½ cups of sugar. Add the desired colour and essence. Mix well. Cover and pressure cook this mixture without adding water. After one whistle reduce the flame and simmer for 45 minutes. If the wheat paste is not cooked well, pressure cook again for another 10 minutes. Let it cool. With a ladle, crush and mash the cooked paste, which is hard, to make it soft and smooth. Heat a heavy-bottomed kadai with 4-5 tsp of ghee. Fry the chopped nuts and pour the paste in this ghee. Cook this paste for 10-15 minutes, stirring continuously till the halwa does not stick to the sides of the kadai. Transfer to a greased tray. Spread evenly. Cut with a greased knife into squares while it is still warm. Decorate with fried chopped nuts.

Note

Wheat halwa can be used for up to 10-15 days. There is no need to store in the refrigerator.

Ukkarai

(STEAMED DHAL)

Ingredients

Moong dhal	*1 cup*
Channa dhal	*1 tbsp*
Powdered jaggery	*1½ cups*
Grated coconut	*1 cup*
Ghee	*2 tbsp*
Cardamom powder	*a pinch*
Saffron	*a pinch*
Cashew nuts	*a few*

Method

Dry roast both dhals and soak in water for 1 hour. Grind to a smooth paste. Steam cook in idli plates till cooked well. Allow to cool and break into fine pieces. In a heavy-bottomed kadai, prepare a thick jaggery syrup of gathering consistency. Mix in coconut and then steamed dhal paste. Add ghee and shallow fry on a low flame till the moisture is totally absorbed and dhal paste and jaggery are well blended. Add cardamom powder, saffron and cashew nuts.

Thengai Burfi

(COCONUT CAKE)

Ingredients for 15 pieces

Grated coconut	*2 cups*
Sugar	*1½ cups*
Rava	*1 tbsp*
Cardamom powder	*1 tsp*
Ghee	*as required*

Method

Dissolve sugar in half cup water, add 1 tbsp of ghee. Mix in coconut. Cook together on a low flame, stirring continuously, till it blends well with sugar. Mix rava, 1 tsp ghee and cardamom powder. Stir together for a few more minutes till it does not stick to the sides of the kadai. Transfer immediately to a greased tray and spread evenly. Cut with a greased knife into squares while the mixture is still warm. Allow to cool. Allow burfis to harden and serve.

Puttu

(STEAMED RICE FLOUR)

Ingredients

Processed rice flour	*3 cups*
Powdered jaggery	*2 cups*
Grated coconut	*3 tbsp*
Cardamom powder	*a pinch*
Roasted cashew nuts	*1 tbsp*
Ghee	*1 tbsp*

Method

Dry roast rice flour to a light pinkish colour. After cooling, sprinkle warm water and mix the flour carefully to a semi-wet consistency. Lay a thin muslin cloth on an idli plate and spread the wet flour evenly on it. Cover it with another thin cloth and then steam cook in an idli cooker. When steamed well, transfer to a dry tray and allow to cool. Prepare a jaggery syrup of three-string consistency. Add ghee. Slowly mix the steamed flour into the syrup, stirring constantly. Turn off the flame. Then add roasted cashew nuts, grated coconut and cardamom powder and mix well. Serve after puttu is cooled to room temperature.

Somas, Karjjikai (Andhra)

Ingredients for the dough for 12 somas

Maida	*¼ cup*
Rava	*1 cup*
Ghee	*1 tsp*
Oil	*for deep frying*

Sieve maida, knead with rava, ghee and enough water to form a soft stiff dough (need not be kneaded too much). Keep aside for 15 minutes covered with a wet cloth.

For filling

Fried gram	*1 cup*
Grated coconut	*2 tbsp*
Powdered sugar	*1½ cups*
Poppy seeds	*1 tbsp*
Cashew nuts	*10*
Cardamom powder	*1 tsp*

Dry roast the poppy seeds in hot kadai, add and roast fried gram, cashew nuts and coconut. Grind to a coarse powder in the mixie (without water). Mix together all the other ingredients in a bowl and keep aside.

To prepare somas

Divide the dough into small balls. Roll out into thin rotis. Keep 1 tbsp of filling in the middle of each roti. Wet the edges with a little water. Fold in half into a semi-circle and seal the edges firmly. Trim the edges with a somas cutter or a sharp knife. Heat oil in a kadai and deep fry somas one by one till light golden brown.

Note

Instead of roasted coconut, 'copra' can be used.

Thengai Burfi

Mysore Pak

Mysore Pak

(CHANNA DHAL FLOUR CAKES)

Ingredients for 15 pieces

Channa dhal flour	*1 cup*
Sugar	*2 cups*
Ghee	*2 cups*

Method

Sift the flour well. Keep aside. In a heavy-bottomed kadai, prepare sugar syrup till one-string consistency. Add half cup ghee to it. Sprinkle the flour gradually into the syrup with one hand, while constantly stirring it with the other hand using a flat ladle. When the flour and syrup mix well, add the remaining ghee gradually, stirring all the while. When the mixture is cooked well and froths up, turn off the flame and immediately transfer to a greased tray. Spread evenly and allow to cool for some time. When the ghee is absorbed completely and small holes appear on top, cut with a greased knife into squares. Store in an airtight container.

Badhusha

Ingredients for 10-12 pieces

Maida	*1 cup*
Sugar	*1 cup*
Cooking soda	*1 tsp*
Kesari colour	*a pinch*
Desired essence	*a few drops*
Ghee or butter	*1 tbsp*
Fresh firm curd	*1 tbsp, optional*
Oil	*for deep frying*
To decorate	
Saffron	*a pinch*
Chopped nuts	*1 tbsp*

Method

Mix ghee and soda in a plate. Rub well with the palm till it becomes flaky. Sift maida and sprinkle on this. Slowly mix well with fingertips till the mixture blends well. Add colour. Add required water (or fresh curd) and knead to a soft dough (do not over knead). To test, flatten a little dough in the palm. If the edges crack, knead again with a little more water. Divide the dough into small balls. Flatten out into ¼" thick rounds in the palm. Make a deep depression in the centre with a finger (do not pierce a hole). Likewise, prepare all the badhushas and arrange on a tray. Heat oil in a kadai to a moderate temperature. Deep fry the badhushas one by one on a low flame, for about 10 minutes, till done. Remove and drain the excess oil on oil absorbent paper. Meanwhile, prepare sugar syrup to one-string consistency. Add the essence and turn off the flame. Dip the prepared badhushas one by one for 1 minute in the sugar syrup with a perforated ladle. Arrange on a tray side by side. Decorate with chopped nuts and saffron immediately.

Kunjaladu

(CHANNA DHAL BALLS)

Ingredients for 10 balls

Channa dhal flour	*1 cup*
Rice flour	*1 tsp*
Baking soda	*a pinch*
Sugar	*1½ cups*
Edible yellow colour	*a pinch*
Oil	*for frying*
To flavour	
Saffron	*a pinch*
Borneal flakes and nutmeg	*a little*
Cloves	*5, powdered*
Cardamom	*5, powdered*
Fried cashew nuts	*5*
Diamond sugar candy	*2 tsp*
Raisins	*1 tsp*

Method

Sift and mix channa dhal flour, rice flour and baking soda in a bowl. Prepare a thick batter with required water. Heat oil in a shallow kadai. Hold the boondhi ladle close to the oil. Pour the batter on it and rub vigorously with a spoon so that very tiny balls 'boondhis' fall into the oil. Deep fry to a golden brown colour. Remove and drain oil completely. Meanwhile, keep the sugar syrup ready. Boil sugar with half cup water, add colour and saffron. When the sugar syrup attains one-string consistency, turn off the flame. Transfer the required amount of hot boondhis into the syrup as soon as they are fried and turn over and mix carefully with a wooden ladle. When the 'boondhi' mixture is cool enough, add all powdered flavouring agents, sugar candy, fried cashew nuts and raisins. Mix well again and roll into small balls.

Porivilangai Urundai

(HARD DHAL AND RICE BALLS)

Ingredients

Channa dhal	*1 cup*
Moong dhal	*1 cup*
Raw rice	*1 cup*
Wheat flour	*1 cup*
Coconut pieces	*1 tbsp*
Dark brown sticky jaggery	*3 cups, powdered*
Cardamom powder	*1 tsp*

Method

Dry roast channa dhal, moong dhal and rice to a light pinkish colour. Pound together in a flour mill to a smooth flour. Dry roast wheat flour also. In a tray mix together coconut pieces, wheat flour, cardamom powder and pounded flour. Keep aside. Prepare jaggery syrup to a soft ball consistency. Slowly pour this syrup (using a spoon) on the flour in the tray, stirring continuously. When the jaggery flour mixture is still warm roll into small balls and arrange in an airtight container. The special feature of this sweet is that there is no ghee at all.

Kadali Urundai

(PEANUT BALLS)

Ingredients for 20 balls

Roasted peanuts	*2 cups*
Powdered dark brown sticky jaggery	*1 cup*

Method

Remove husk from peanuts. Prepare a jaggery syrup of soft ball consistency. Turn off the flame. Add peanuts into the syrup and mix well. When it is still hot, roll into small balls.

Note

Rub a little rice flour on the hands so that the jaggery does not stick.

Pottukadali Urundai

(FRIED GRAM BALLS)

Method

This is prepared in the same way as peanut balls, using fried gram instead of peanuts.

Karthigai Pori

(PUFFED RICE BALLS)

Ingredients for 10 balls

Puffed rice or rice flakes	*2 cups*
Fried gram	*2 tbsp*
Dark sticky jaggery	*1 cup*
Coconut pieces	*1 tbsp*
Roasted peanuts	*1 tbsp*

Method

Mix all ingredients except jaggery in a large bowl. Prepare a thick jaggery syrup till a soft ball consistency is attained. Pour the syrup gradually into the bowl loosely and mix quickly (add only required syrup). When it is still hot, roll into big balls between the hands. This is prepared especially on a festival called Karthigai which is the Hindu god Karthikeya's birthday.

Note

Rub a little rice flour in the hands so that the jaggery does not stick.

Maaladu

(DHAL POWDER BALLS)

Ingredients for 20 balls

Roasted moong dhal or fried gram	*2 cups (200 gms)*
Sugar	*1½ cups (150 gms)*
Ghee	*1 cup*
Roasted cashew nuts	*1 tsp*
Cardamom powder	*a pinch*

Method

Grind moong dhal and sugar to a very fine powder and mix well. Add cardamom powder and cashew nuts. Melt ghee and pour into it. When it is still hot, prepare into small balls.

Rava Ladu

(RAVA BALLS)

Method

Grind rava to a fine powder and continue in the same way as maaladu.

Adhirasam

Ingredients

Processed rice flour	*2 cups*
Dark brown sticky jaggery	*1 cup, powdered*
Cardamom powder	*1 tsp*
Sesame seeds	*1 tsp, optional*
Oil	*for deep frying*
Milk	*a little*

Method

Sieve the rice flour and spread it in a large shallow plate. In a heavy-bottomed vessel, prepare jaggery syrup to a soft ball consistency. Add cardamom powder. Pour the required amount of syrup slowly over the flour, stirring continuously with a ladle till it forms a thick dough (or sprinkle small amounts of flour quickly into the syrup and stir continuously). Mix in sesame seeds, put a little oil on the dough, cover, and leave the dough for a minimum of one day. Just before preparing, sprinkle a little milk on the dough and knead it into a soft dough again. Divide into small balls and flatten into a circle over a greased plastic sheet or plantain leaf. Heat oil in a shallow kadai and reduce the flame. Deep fry each adhirasam one by one to a dark golden brown colour. Drain excess oil completely by pressing well with a flat ladle.

Arrange them on a tray side by side so that they do not stick to each other.

Note

This is supposed to be an auspicious sweet prepared on festival days like Deepavali and is a must during weddings in southern states.

It can be stored for 15-20 days.

Manoharam

(CRISPY SWEET MURUKKU)

Ingredients

Processed rice flour	*2 cups*
Roasted urad dhal flour	*3 tsp*
Dark brown sticky jaggery	*200 gms*
Butter or ghee	*a little*
Salt	*to taste*
Oil	*for deep frying*

Method

Mix together rice flour, urad dhal flour, 1 tsp of butter and a pinch of salt. Sprinkle water gradually and prepare a stiff dough. Divide into small cylindrical balls. Meanwhile, heat oil in kadai. Stuff each ball into the murukku maker with the specified mould plate and press in a circular motion in the hot oil. Deep fry till they turn golden brown and remove, draining the oil completely. Break the prepared manoharam into small pieces and spread on a tray. Keep aside. In a separate kadai, prepare a stiff jaggery syrup of a soft ball consistency. Pour this syrup over the manoharam pieces slowly. Mix well and when it is still hot, shape it into big balls between the hands. As and when the syrup becomes cold, it may be reheated mildly. Store in an airtight container.

Note

Rub hands with a little rice flour so that the syrup does not stick.

Manoharam

Rava Thulli

Vella Cheedai

(CRISP RICE BALLS)

Ingredients

Processed rice flour	*1 cup*
Roasted urad dhal flour	*1½ tsp*
White sesame seeds	*1 tsp*
Small thin coconut pieces	*1 tsp*
Cardamom powder	*a pinch*
Powdered dark sticky jaggery	*1 cup*
Oil	*for deep frying*

Method

Dry roast the rice flour in a hot pan for 2-3 minutes. (To test whether the flour is roasted properly, hold a pinch between the thumb and forefinger. Draw a line with it on the floor. The line should fall continuously without any breaks.) Sift the roasted flour through a fine sieve. Dissolve the jaggery in 1 cup water and heat till it attains a soft ball consistency. Add coconut bits and slowly add the roasted flour, stirring constantly with a ladle. Cook for 5 minutes till the dough can be rolled in your fingers. Transfer to a plate and allow to cool. Mix roasted dhal flour and knead into a smooth, firm dough. If required, a little warm water can be sprinkled. Divide and roll into small rough balls and spread on a cloth. Deep fry in moderately hot oil till the balls turn brown.

Note

This dough can be used on the same day, after cooling, or can be kept for one day and then used.

Rava Thulli

(RAVA KESARI)

Ingredients

Fine rava	*1 cup*
Sugar	*1 cup*
Edible yellow colour	*a pinch*
Cardamom powder	*½ tsp*
Ghee	*2 tbsp*
Cashew nuts and raisins	*to decorate*

Method

Shallow fry rava in a little ghee in a hot kadai for 2 minutes. Boil 2 cups of water, adding colour, a little ghee, and cardamom powder. Add the fried rava in the boiling water, stirring continuously, cook rava completely (if required, water can be sprinkled). Add sugar, stirring till the sugar dissolves and mix well. Cook together for a few minutes, add a little ghee. Cook on low flame till it does not stick to the sides and gets a shine. Transfer to a greased tray, spread evenly and decorate with nuts.

Guide To Measurements In The Book

Abbreviations	
gm	gram
kg	kilogram
ml	millilitre
tsp	teaspoon
tbsp	tablespoon

Working Approximates	
1 medium potato	75 gm
1 medium onion	50 gm
1 medium tomato	50 gm
1" ginger	10 gm

Metric-Imperial Conversion Chart (working approximates)	
Metric	**US/Imperial**
450 gm	1lb
1000 gm/1kg	2.2lb
30 gm	1 oz
1000ml/1litre	2 pints

Cup and Spoon Measures	
1 tsp	5 gm
1 tbsp/3tsp	15 gm
1 tbsp/3tsp	15 ml
1 cup	40gm /8oz/16 tbsp

Cup measures for various ingredients (working approximates)	
Ingredients	**1 cup**
All flour (rice flour, wheat flour)	100-120gm
All pulses (toor dhal, urad dhal)	180-200gm
All dry beans (chick peas, dry peas)	180-200gm
Rice	180-200gm
All liquids (milk, water, oils)	180-200ml
Sugar/jaggery	140-160gm

Glossary

Vegetables

ENGLISH	HINDI	TAMIL
Ash gourd	Ghiya	Pooshanikkai
Banana (raw	Kaccha kela	Vazhakkai
Beans (broad	Bakla, sem	Avarai
Beans (cluster)	Gwar- ki- phalli	Kothavarangai
Bitter gourd	Karela	Pavakkai
Bitterberry	Asheta	Sundakkai
Bottle gourd	Dodhi, lauki	Suraikai
Brinjal	Baingan	Kathirikkai
Cabbage	Bandh gobi	Muttaikos
Cauliflower	Phool gobi	Cauliflower
Carrot	Gajar	Carrot
Capsicum/bell pepper	Simla mirch	Kudamilagai
Citron (bitter)	Khatta, nimbu	Narthangai
Coconut	Nariyal	Thengai
Coconut (dry)	Copra	Kopparai
Coconut (tender)	Dab	Elaneer
Colocasia	Arbi	Seppam kizhangu
Cucumber	Kheera, kakadi	Vellarikkai
Drumstick	Swanjan	Murungakkai
Elephant yam	Suran, jamikand	Senai kizhangu
Fenugreek leaves	Methi	Venthiya keerai`
Greens	Amaranth	Mulai keerai
Gherkins	Kundru, Tendil	Kovakkai
Gooseberry	Amla	Nellikkai
Lime leaves	Nimbu-ka-patha	Narthella
Lotus stem	Kamal Kakri	Thamara thandu
Lotus root	Kamal-ki-jadh	Thamara Kizhangu
Ladies finger	Bhindi	Vendakkai
Mango (raw)	Aam (kacha)	Mangai
Mango (tender)	-	Vadumangai
Mint	Pudhina	Pudhina
Mushroom	Dhingri	Kaalan
Mustard greens	Sarson-ka-sag	Kadugu ilai
Neem flower	Neem-ka-phool	Vepampoo
Neem leaves, margosa	Neem-ke-patte	Veppilai
Onion	Pyaaz	Periya vengayam
Onion (small), shallots	Pyaaz	Chinna vengayam,
–	–	sambar vengayam
Peas	Mattar	Pachai pattani
Potato	Aalu	Urilai kizhangu
Radish	Mooli	Mullangi

ENGLISH	HINDI	TAMIL
Ridge gourd	Tori	Peerkangai
Snake gourd	Chachinda, padual	Pudalangai
Spinach	Palak	Pasalai keerai
Spring onion	Hara pyaaz	Vengaya thal
Sweet potato	Shakarkand	Sakaravalli
–	–	Kizhangu
Tapioca	Saabudhaana	Maravalli kizhangu
Tomato	Tamatar	Thakkalli
Yam	Sooran	Pidikarunai

Fruits

ENGLISH	HINDI	TAMIL
Banana (ripe)	Kela	Vazhapazham
–	Jamoon	Naval pazham
Custard apple	Sitaphul	Sita pazham
Grapes	Angoor	Draksha
Guava	Amrud	Koyyapazham
Jackfruit (ripe)	Kathal	Pala pazham
Lemon, lime	Nimbu	Elumichampazham
Mango (ripe)	Aam (pakka)	Mambazham
Musk melon	Kharbooja	Kirni pazham
Orange	Santra	Orange, Kichilli
–	–	Pazham
Papaya	Papita	Pappali
Pear	Nashpati	Berikai
Pineapple	Ananas	Anasi pazham
Pomegranate	Anar	Mathulam pazham
Sweet lemon	Musambi	Sathukudi
Watermelon	Tarbuj	Darbusini
Woodapple	Kaith	Vilam pazham

Condiments And Spices

ENGLISH	HINDI	TAMIL
Aniseed	Saunf	Perumjeerakam
Asafoetida	Hing	Perungayam
Bay leaves	Tej pattha	Brinji ilai
Cardamom	Elaichi	Elakai
Cinnamon	Dalchini	Lavangapattai
Cloves	Lavang	Krambu
Chillies (green)	Hari mirch	Pachai milagai
Chillies (dry, red)	Lal mirch	Milagai vatral

ENGLISH	HINDI	TAMIL
Cumin seeds	Jeera	Jeeragam
Carum, tymol	Ajwain	Omum
Coriander leaves, cilantro	Hara dhania	Kothamalli
Coriander seeds	Dhania	Kothamaliverai
Curry leaves	Curri patta	Kariveppilai
Fenugreek seeds	Methi	Venthayam
Fennel seeds	Saunf	Sombu
Garlic	Lassan	Ullipoondu
Ginger (fresh)	Adrak	Inji
Ginger (dry)	Saunth	Chukku
Kandanthippilli	Pipal	Kadugu
Mace	Javithri	Jathipatri
Mango powder (dry)	Amchoor	Mangai podi
Nutmeg	Jaiphal	Jaathikkai
Onion seeds, black cumin seeds	Kalonji, kalajeera	Karunjeeragam
Pepper corns	Kalimirch	Milagu
Poppy seeds	Khus-khus	Khasakhasa
Saffron	Kesar	Kungumappu
Sesame seeds	Til	Ellu
Turmeric	Haldi	Manjal

Miscellaneous

ENGLISH	HINDI	TAMIL
Almond	Badaam	Badaam
Areca nut	Supari	Pakku
Bengal gram	Chane-ki-dhal	Kadalai paruppu
Bengal gram (whole)	Kala channa	Kothukadalai
Black gram	Urad dhal	Ulutham paruppu
Black gram (whole)	Urad	Muzlu ulundu
Butter	Makkhan	Vennai
Buttermilk	Lassi	Moru
Bengal gram flour	Besan	Kadalai mavu
Barley Jau	Barli	arisi
Betel leaves	Pan-ke-patte	Vethilai
Cashew nuts	Kaju	Mundhiri paruppu
Chickpeas	Kabuli channa	Konda kadalai
Cow peas	Lobia	Karamani
Curds	Dahi	Thayir
Cottage cheese	Paneer	Paal katti
Date	Khajoor	Pericham pazham
Field beans	Val	Mocchakottai
Red kidney beans	Rajmah	Rajmah
Fried gram, roasted gram	Bhunna channa	Pottu kadalai
Ghee	Ghee	Nei
Gingelly oil	Til thel	Nalla yennai
Green gram (whole)	Moong	Pasipayir

ENGLISH	HINDI	TAMIL
Green gram	Moong dhal	Payatham
–	–	paruppu
Groundnut, peanuts	Moong phalli	Nilakkadalai
Honey	Shaihd	Then
Horse gram	Kulthi	Kollu
Hydrogenated oil	Vanaspathi	Vanaspathi
Italian millet	Kangni	Thenai
Jaggery	Ghur	Vellam
Jowar, sorghum	Jowar	Cholam
Khesari gram	Kesari dhal	Khesari paruppu
Red lentil	Masur dhal	Mysore paruppu
Moth beans	Moth	Narippayir
Milk (buffalo)	Bhains-ka-doodh	Erumai paal
Milk (cow)	Gai-ka-doodh	Pasum paal
Maize, corn	Makki	Makka cholam
Pearl millet, bajra	Bajra	Cambu
Ragi	Madua	Kezhvaragu
Raisins, currant	Kismis	Kaintha dhraatchai
Red gram	Thoor dhal	Thuvaram
–	–	paruppu
Refined flour	Maida	Maida mavu
Rice (parboiled)	Usnachawal	Puzhungal arisi
Rice (raw)	Chawal	Arisi
Rice (beaten/flakes)	Chewra, poha	Aval
Rice (puffed)	Bhel	Arisi Pori
Salt	Namak	Uppu
Salt (rock)	Kala namak	Kal uppu
Sago	Saabudhaana	Jevvarisi
Semolina, cream of wheat	Rava, sooji	Ravai
Sugar candy	–	Kalkandu
Sugar syrup	Sheera	Chakkarai paagu
Sugarcane	Ganna, sherdi	Karumbu
Tamarind	Imli	Puli
–	Kodra	Varagu
Vermicelli	Sewian	Semiya
Wheat	Gehun	Godhumai
Whole wheat flour	Atta	Godhumai maavu